MAN'S FOURFOLD STATE.

STATE I.—THE STATE OF INNOCENCE.

II. THE STATE OF NATURE.

III. THE STATE OF GRACE.

PART 1.—ON REGENERATION.

1 Pet. i. 23.—Being born again, not of corruptible seed, but of incorruptible, by the word of God, which liveth and abideth for ever, ... 138

PART 2.—MYSTICAL UNION BETWEEN CHRIST AND BELIEVERS.

John xv. 5 —I am the vine, ye are the branches, ... 177

IV. THE ETERNAL STATE.

STATE III.

THE STATE OF GRACE.

PART I.

ON REGENERATION.

1 Peter i. 23,

Being born again, not of corruptible seed, but of incorruptible, by the word of God, which liveth and abideth for ever.

We proceed now to the state of grace, the state of begun recovery of human nature, into which all that shall partake of eternal happiness are translated, sooner or later, while in this world. It is the result of a gracious change made upon those who shall inherit eternal life: which change may be taken up in these two particulars: 1. In opposition to their natural real state, the state of corruption, there is a change made upon them in regeneration; whereby their nature is changed. 2. In opposition to their natural relative state, the state of wrath, there is a change made upon them in their union with the Lord Jesus Christ; by which they are placed beyond the reach of condemnation. These, therefore, regeneration and union with Christ, I desire to treat on as the great and comprehensive changes on a sinner, bringing him into the state of grace.

The first of these we have in the text; together with the outward and ordinary means by which it is brought about. The apostle here, to excite the saints to the study of holiness, and particularly of brotherly love, puts them in mind of their spiritual original. He tells them that they were born again; and that of incorruptible seed, the word of God. This shows them to be brethren, partakers of the same new nature: which is the root from which holiness, and particularly brotherly love, springs. We have been once born sinners: we must be born again, that we may be saints. The simple word signifies "to be begotten;" and so it may be read, Matth. xi. 11; "to be conceived," Matt. i. 20; and "to be born," Matt. ii. 1. Accordingly, the compound word, used in the text, may be taken in its full latitude, the last idea presupposing the two former: so regeneration is a supernatural real change on the whole man, fitly compared to the natural birth, as will afterwards appear. The ordinary means of regeneration, called the "seed," whereof the new creature is formed, is not corruptible seed. Of such, indeed our bodies are generated: but the spiritual seed of which the new creature is generated, is incorruptible; namely, "the word of God, which liveth and abideth for ever." The sound of the word of God passeth, even as other sounds do; but the word lasteth, liveth, and abideth, in respect of its everlasting effects, on all upon whom it operates. This "word, which by the gospel is preached unto you," ver. 25, impregnated by the Spirit of God, is the means of regeneration: and by it dead sinners are raised to life.

DOCTRINE. All men in the state of grace, are born again. All gracious persons, namely, such as are in a state of favour with God, and endowed with gracious qualities and dispositions, are regenerate persons. In discoursing on this subject, I shall shew, What regeneration is; next, Why it is so called; and then apply the doctrine.

I. Of the Nature of regeneration.

For the better understanding of the nature of regeneration, take this along with you, that as there are false conceptions in nature, so there are also in grace: by these many are deluded, mistaking some partial changes made upon them, for this great and thorough change. To remove such mistakes, let these few things be considered: (1.) Many call the church their mother, whom God will not own to be his children, Cant. i. 6. "My mother's children," that is, false brethren, "were angry with me." All that are baptized, are not born again. Simon was baptized, yet still "in the gall of bitterness, and in the bond of iniquity," Acts viii. 13, 23. Where Christianity is the religion of the country, many are called by the name of Christ, who have no more of him than the name: and no wonder, for the devil had his goats among Christ's sheep, in those places where but few professed the Christian religion, 1 John ii. 19, "They went out from us, but they were not of us." (2.) Good education is not regeneration. Education may chain up men's lusts, but cannot change their hearts. A wolf is still a ravenous beast, though it be in chains. Joash was very devout during the life of his good tutor Jehoiada; but afterwards he quickly shewed what spirit he was of, by his sudden apostasy, 2 Chron. xxiv. 2—18. Good example is of mighty influence to change the outward man: but that change often goes off, when a man changes his company; of which the world affords many sad instances. (3.) A turning from open profanity, to civility and sobriety, falls short of this saving change. Some are, for a while, very loose, especially in their younger years; but at length they reform, and leave their profane courses. Here is a change, yet only such as may be found in men utterly void of the grace of God, and whose righteousness is so far from exceeding, that it doth not come up to the righteousness of the Scribes and Pharisees. (4.) One may engage in all the outward duties of religion, and yet not be born again. Though lead be cast into various shapes, it remains still but a base metal. Men may escape the pollutions of the world, and yet be but dogs and swine, 2 Pet. ii. 20—22. All the external acts of religion are within the compass of natural abilities. Yea, hypocrites may have the counterfeit of all the graces of the Spirit: for we read of "true holiness," Eph. iv. 24; and "faith unfeigned," 1 Tim. i. 5; which shews us that there is counterfeit holiness, and a feigned faith. (5.) Men may advance to a great deal of strictness in their own way of religion, and yet be strangers to the new birth, Acts xxvi. 5, "After the most straitest sect of our religion, I lived a Pharisee." Nature has its own unsanctified strictness in religion. The Pharisees had so much of it, that they looked on Christ as little better than a mere libertine. A man whose conscience has been awakened, and who lives under the felt influence of the covenant of works, what will he not do that is within the compass of natural abilities? It is a truth, though it came out of a hellish mouth, that "skin for skin, yea all that a man hath will he give for his life," Job ii. 4. (6.) A person may have sharp soul-exercises and pangs, and yet die in the birth. Many "have been in pain," that have but, "as it were, brought forth wind." There may be sore pangs of conscience, which turn to nothing at last. Pharaoh and Simon Magus had such convictions, as made them to desire the prayers of others for them. Judas repented himself: and, under terrors of conscience, gave back his ill-gotten pieces of silver. All is not gold that glitters. Trees may blossom fairly in the spring, on which no fruit is to be found in the harvest: and some have sharp soul-exercises, which are nothing but foretastes of hell.

The new birth, however in appearance hopefully begun, may be marred two ways. Some have sharp convictions for a while: but these go off, and they become as careless about their salvation, and as profane as ever, and usually worse than ever; "their last state is worse than their first," Matt. xii. 45. They get awakening grace, but not converting grace; and that goes off by degrees, as the light of the declining day, till it issues in midnight darkness. Others come forth too soon; they are born, like Ishmael, before the time of the promise, Gen. xvi. 2; compare Gal. iv. 22, &c. They take up with a mere law work, and stay not till the time of the promise of the gospel. They snatch at consolation, not waiting till it be given them; and foolishly draw their comfort from the law that wounded them. They apply the healing plaster to themselves, before their wound, is sufficiently searched. The law, that rigorous husband, severely beats them, and throws in curses and vengeance upon their souls; then they fall to reforming, praying, mourning, promising, and vowing, till this ghost be laid; which done, they fall asleep again in the arms of the law: but they are never shaken out of themselves and their own righteousness, nor brought forward to Jesus Christ. There may be a wonderful moving of the affections, in souls that are not at all touched with regenerating grace. When there is no grace, there may, notwithstanding, be a flood of tears, as in Esau, who "found no place of repentance, though he sought it carefully with tears," Heb. xii. 17. There may be great flashes of joy; as in the hearers of the word, represented in the parable of the stony ground, who "anon with joy receive it," Matt. xiii. 20. There may be also great desires after good things, and great delight in them too; as in those hypocrites described in Isa. lviii. 2, "Yet they seek me daily, and delight to know my ways:—they take delight in approaching to God."—See how high they may sometimes stand, who yet fall away, Heb. vi. 4—6. They may be "enlightened, taste of the heavenly gift," "be partakers of the Holy Ghost, taste the good word of God, and the powers of the world to come." Common operations of the divine Spirit, like a land-flood, make a strange turning of things upside down: but when they are over, all runs again in the ordinary channel. All these things may be, where the sanctifying Spirit of Christ never rests upon the soul, but the stony heart still remains; and in that case these affections cannot but wither, because they have no root.

But regeneration is a real, thorough change, whereby the man is made a new creature, 2 Cor. v. 17. The Lord God makes the creature a new creature, as the goldsmith melts down a vessel of dishonour, and makes it a vessel of honour. Man is, in respect of his spiritual state, altogether disjointed by the fall; every faculty of the soul is, as it were, dislocated: in regeneration, the Lord loosens every joint, and sets it right again. Now this change made in regeneration, is,

1. A change of qualities or dispositions: it is not a change of the substance, but of the qualities of the soul. Vicious qualities are removed, and the contrary dispositions are brought in, in their room. "The old man is put off," Eph. iv. 22; "the new man is put on," ver. 24. Man lost none of the rational faculties of his soul by sin: he had an understanding still, but it was darkened; he had still a will, but it was contrary to the will of God. So in regeneration, there is not a new substance created, but new qualities are infused; light instead of darkness, righteousness instead of unrighteousness.

2. It is a supernatural change; he that is born again, is born of the Spirit, John iii. 5. Great changes may be made by the power of nature, especially when assisted by external revelation. Nature may be so elevated by the common influences of the Spirit, that a person may thereby be turned into another man, as Saul was, 1 Sam. x. 6, who yet never becomes a new man. But in regeneration, nature itself is changed, and we become partakers of the divine nature; and this must needs be a supernatural change. How can we, who are dead in trespasses and sins, renew ourselves, any more than a dead man can raise himself out of his grave? Who but the sanctifying Spirit of Christ can form Christ in a soul, changing it into the same image? Who but the Spirit of sanctification can give the new heart? Well may we say, when we see a man thus changed, "This is the finger of God!"

3. It is a change into the likeness of God, 2 Cor. iii. 18, "We—beholding, as in a glass, the glory of the Lord, are changed into the same image." Every thing generates its like: the child bears the image of the parent; and they who are born of God, bear God's image. Man aspiring to be as God, made himself like the devil. In his natural state he resembles the devil, as a child doth his father, John viii. 44, "Ye are of your father the devil." But when this happy change comes, that image of Satan is defaced, and the image of God is restored. Christ himself, who is the brightness of his Father's glory, is the pattern after which the new creature is made, Rom. viii. 29, "For whom he did foreknow, he also did predestinate to be conformed to the image of his Son." Hence he is said to be formed in the regenerate, Gal. iv. 19.

4. It is a universal change; "all things become new," 2 Cor. v. 17. It is a blessed leaven, that leavens the whole lump, the whole spirit, and soul, and body. Original sin infects the whole man; and regenerating grace, which is the cure, goes as far as the disease. This fruit of the Spirit is in all goodness; goodness of the mind, goodness of the will, goodness of the affections, goodness of the whole man. He gets not only a new head, to know religion, or a new tongue, to talk of it; but a new heart, to love and embrace it, in the whole of his conversation. When the Lord opens the sluice of grace, on the soul's new-birth day, the waters run through the whole man, to purify and make him fruitful. In those natural changes spoken of before, there are, as it were, pieces of new cloth put into an old garment; new life to an old heart: but the gracious change is a thorough change; a change both of heart and life.

Yet, though every part of the man is renewed, there is no part of him perfectly renewed. As an infant has all the parts of a man but none of them come to a perfect growth; so regeneration brings a perfection of parts, to be brought forward in the gradual advances of sanctification, 1 Pet. ii. 2, "As new-born babes, desire the sincere milk of the word, that ye may grow thereby." Although, in regeneration, there is heavenly light let into the mind; yet there is still some darkness there: though the will is renewed, it is not perfectly renewed; there is still some of the old inclination to sin remaining: and thus it will be, till that which is in part is done away, and the light of glory come. Adam was created at his full stature; but those who are born, must have their time to grow up; so those who are born again, come forth into the new world of grace as new-born babes: Adam being created upright, was at the same time perfectly righteous, without the least mixture of sinful imperfection.

6. Nevertheless, it is a lasting change, which never goes off. The seed is incorruptible, saith the text; and so is the creature that is formed of it. The life given in regeneration, whatever decays it may fall under, can never be utterly lost. "His seed remaineth in him" who "is born of God," 1 John iii. 9. Though the branches should be cut down, the root abides in the earth; and being watered with the dew of heaven, shall sprout again: for "the root of the righteous shall not be moved," Prov. xii. 3. But to come to particulars.

1. In regeneration the mind is savingly enlightened. There is a light let into the understanding; so that they who were "some time darkness, are now light in the Lord," Ephes. v. 8. The beams of the light of life make their way into the dark dungeon of the heart: then the night is over, and the morning light is come, which will shine more and more unto the perfect day. Now the man is illuminated,

(1.) In the knowledge of God. He has far other thoughts of God, than ever he had before, Hos. ii. 20, "I will even betrothe thee unto me in faithfulness, and thou shalt know the Lord." The Spirit of the Lord brings him back to this question, "What is God?" and catechises him anew upon that grand point, so that he is made to say, "I have heard of thee by the hearing of the ear; but now mine eye seeth thee," Job xlii. 5. The spotless purity of God, his exact justice, his all-sufficiency, and other glorious perfections revealed in his word, are by this new light discovered to the soul, with a plainness and certainty, which as far exceed the knowledge it had of these things before, as ocular demonstration exceeds common report. For now he sees what he only heard of before.

(2.) He is enlightened in the knowledge of sin. He has different thoughts of it than he used to have. Formerly his sight could not pierce through the cover Satan laid over it: but now the Spirit of God removes it, wipes off the paint and varnish; and so he sees it in its natural colours, as the worst of evils, exceedingly sinful, Rom. vii. 13. O what deformed monsters do formerly beloved lusts appear! Were they right eyes, he would pluck them out; were they right hands, he would consent to their being cut off. He sees how offensive sin is to God, how destructive it is to the soul; and calls himself a fool, for fighting so long against the Lord, and harbouring that destroyer as a bosom friend.

(3.) He is instructed in the knowledge of himself. Regenerating grace brings the prodigal to himself, Luke xv. 17, and makes men full of eyes within, knowing every one the plague of his own heart. The mind being savingly enlightened, the man sees how desperately corrupt his nature is; what enmity against God, and his holy law, has long lodged there: so that his soul loathes itself. No open sepulchre so vile and loathsome, in his eyes, as himself, Ezek. xxxvi. 31, "Then shall ye remember your own evil ways, and your doings that were not good, and shall loathe yourselves in your own sight." He is no worse than he was before: but the sun is shining; and so those pollutions are seen, which he could not discern, when there was no dawning in him, as the word is, Isa. viii. 20, while as yet there was no breaking of the day of grace with him.

(4.) He is enlightened in the knowledge of Jesus Christ. 1 Cor. i. 23, 24, "But we preach Christ crucified, unto the Jews a stumbling-block, and unto the Greeks foolishness: but unto them which are called, both Jews and Greeks, Christ the power of God, and the wisdom of God." The truth is, unregenerate men, though capable of preaching Christ, have not, properly speaking, the knowledge of him, but only an opinion, a good opinion, of him; as one has of many controverted points of doctrine, wherein he is far from certainty. As when you meet with a stranger on the road, who behaves himself discretely, you conceive a good opinion of him, and therefore willingly converse with him: but yet you will not commit your money to him; because, though you have a good opinion of the man, he is a stranger to you, you do not know him: so may they think well of Christ; but they will never commit themselves to him, seeing they know him not. But saving illumination carries the soul beyond opinion, to the certain knowledge of Christ and his excellency, 1 Thess. i. 5, "For our Gospel came not unto you in word only, but also in power, and in the Holy Ghost, and in much assurance." The light of grace thus discovers the suitableness of the mystery of Christ to the divine perfections, and to the sinner's case. Hence the regenerate admire the glorious plan of salvation, through Christ crucified; rest their whole dependence upon it, heartily acquiesce therein; for whatever he be to others, he is to them "Christ the power of God, and the wisdom of God." But unrenewed men, not seeing this, are offended in him: they will not venture their souls in that vessel, but betake themselves to the broken boards of their own righteousness. The same light convincingly discovers a superlative worth, a transcendent glory and excellence in Christ, which darken all created excellencies as the rising sun makes the stars hide their heads: it engages the "merchantman to sell all that he hath, to buy the one pearl of great price," Matth. xii. 45, 46, makes the soul heartily content to take Christ for all, and instead of all. An unskilful merchant, to whom one offers a pearl of great price, for all his petty wares, dares not venture on the bargain; for though he thinks that one pearl may be worth more than all he has, yet he is not sure of it: but when a jeweller comes to him and assures him it is worth double all his wares, he then eagerly makes the bargain, and cheerfully parts with all he has for that pearl. Finally, this illumination in the knowledge of Christ, convincingly discovers to men a fulness in him, sufficient for the supply of all their wants, enough to satisfy the boundless desires of an immortal soul. And they are persuaded that such fulness is in him, and that in order to be communicated: they depend upon it as a certain truth; and therefore their souls take up their eternal rest in him.

(5.) The man is instructed in the knowledge of the vanity of the world, Psalm cxix. 96, "I have seen an end of all perfection." Regenerating grace elevates the soul, translates it into the spiritual world, from whence this earth cannot but appear a little, yea, a very little thing; even as heaven appeared before, while the soul was grovelling in the earth. Grace brings a man into a new world: where this world is reputed but a stage of vanity, a howling wilderness, a valley of tears. God has hung the sign of vanity at the door of all created enjoyments: yet how do men throng into the house, calling and looking for somewhat that is satisfying; even after it has been a thousand times told them, that there is no such thing in it, it is not to be got there, Isa. lvii. 10, "Thou art wearied in the greatness of thy way: yet saidst thou not, There is no hope." Why are men so foolish? The truth of the matter lies here, they do not see by the light of grace, they do not spiritually discern that sign of vanity. They have often indeed made a rational discovery of it: but can that truly wean the heart from the world? Nay, no more than painted fire can burn off the prisoner's bands.

But the light of grace, is the light of life, powerful and efficacious.

(6.) To sum up all. In regeneration, the mind is enlightened in the knowledge of spiritual things, 1 John ii. 20, "Ye have an unction from the Holy One," that is, from Jesus Christ, Rev. iii. 18. It is an allusion to the sanctuary, whence the holy oil was brought to anoint the priest, "and ye know all things" necessary to salvation. Though men be not book-learned, if they are born again, they are Spirit-learned; for all such are taught of God, John vi. 45. The Spirit of regeneration teaches them what they knew not before and what they knew by the ear only, he teaches them over again as by the eye. The light of grace is an overcoming light, determining men to assent to divine truths on the mere testimony of God. It is no easy thing for the mind of man to acquiesce in divine revelation. Many pretend great respect to the Scriptures; whom, nevertheless, the clear Scripture testimony will not divorce from their preconceived opinions. But this illumination will make men's minds run, as willing captives, after Christ's chariot wheels, which they are ready to allow to drive over, and "cast down" their "imaginations, and every high thing that exalteth itself against the knowledge of God," 2 Cor. x. 5. It will bring them to "receive the kingdom of God as a little child," Mark x. 15, who thinks he has sufficient ground to believe any thing, if his father do but say it is so.

2. The will is renewed. The Lord takes away the stony heart, and gives a heart of flesh, Ezek. xxxvi. 26, and so of stones raiseth up children to Abraham. Regenerating grace is powerful and efficacious, and gives the will a new turn. It does not indeed force it; but sweetly, yet powerfully draws it, so that his people are willing in the day of his power, Psalm cx. 3. There is heavenly oratory in the Mediators lips to persuade sinners, Psalm xlv. 2. "Grace is poured into thy lips." There are cords of a man, and bands of love in his hands, to draw them after him, Hos. xi. 4. Love makes a net for elect souls, which will infallibly catch them, and bring them to land. The cords of Christ's love are strong cords: and they need to be so, for every sinner is heavier than a mountain of brass; and Satan, together with the heart itself, draws the contrary way. But love is strong as death; and the Lord's love to the soul he died for, is the strongest love; which acts so powerfully, that it must come off victorious.

(1.) The will is cured of its utter inability to will what is good. While the opening of the prison to them that are bound, is proclaimed in the gospel, the Spirit of God comes and opens the prison door, goes to the prisoner, and, by the power of his grace, makes his chains fall off; breaks the bonds of iniquity, wherewith he was held in sin, so as he could neither will nor do any thing truly good; brings him forth into a large place, " working in him both to will and to do of his good pleasure," Phil. ii. 13. Then it is that the soul, that was fixed to the earth, can move heavenward; the withered hand is restored, and can be stretched out.

(2.) There is wrought in the will a fixed aversion to evil. In regeneration, a man gets a new spirit put within him, Ezek. xxxvi. 26; and that spirit striveth against the flesh, Gal. v. 17. The sweet morsel of sin, so greedily swallowed down, he now loathes, and would fain be rid of it, even as willingly as one who had drunk a cup of poison would throw it up again. When the spring is stopped, the mud lies in the well unmoved; but when once the spring is cleared, the waters, springing up, will work the mud away by degrees. Even so, while a man continues in an unregenerate state, sin lies at ease in the heart; but as soon as the Lord strikes the rocky heart with the rod of his strength, in the day of conversion, grace is " in him a well of water, springing up into everlasting life," John iv. 14, working away natural corruption, and gradually purifying the heart, Acts xv. 9. The renewed will riseth up against sin, strikes at the root thereof, and the branches too. Lusts are now grievous, and the soul endeavours to starve them; the corrupt nature is the source of all evil, and therefore the soul will be often laying it before the great Physician. O what sorrow, shame, and self-loathing fill the heart, in the day that grace makes its triumphant entrance into it! For now the madman is come to himself, and the remembrance of his follies cannot but cut him to the heart.

(3.) The will is endowed with an inclination, bent, and propensity to good. In its depraved state, it lay quite another way, being prone and bent to evil only: but now, by the operation of the omnipotent, all-conquering arm, it is drawn from evil to good, and gets another turn. As the former was natural, so this is natural too, in regard to the new nature given in regeneration, which has its holy strivings, as well as the corrupt nature has its sinful lustings, Gal. v. 17. The will, as renewed, points towards God and godliness. When God made man, his will, in respect of its intention, was directed towards God, as his chief end; in respect of its choice, it pointed towards that which God willed. When man unmade himself, his will was framed to the very reverse hereof: he made himself his chief end, and his own will his law. But when man is new made, in regeneration, grace rectifies this disorder in some measure, though not perfectly: because we are but renewed in part, while in this world. It brings back the sinner out of himself, to God, as his chief end, Psalm lxxiii. 25, " Whom have I in heaven but thee ?

and there is none upon earth that I desire besides thee." Phil. i. 21, " For me to live is Christ." It makes him to deny himself, and whatever way he turns, to point habitually towards God, who is the centre of the gracious soul, its home, its " dwelling place in all generations," Psalm xc. 1. By regenerating grace, the will is brought into a conformity to the will of God. It is conformed to his preceptive will, being endowed with holy inclinations, agreeable to every one of his commands. The whole law is impressed on the gracious soul : every part of it is written on the renewed heart. Although remaining corruption makes such blots in the writing, that oft-times the man himself cannot read it, yet he that wrote it can read it at all times ; it is never quite blotted out, nor can be. What he has written, he has written ; and it shall stand : " For this is the covenant—I will put my laws into their mind, and write them in their hearts," Heb. viii. 10. It is a covenant of salt, a perpetual covenant. It is also conformed to his providential will; so that the man would no more be master of his own process, nor carve out his lot for himself. He learns to say, from his heart, " The will of the Lord be done." " He shall choose our inheritance for us," Psalm xlvii. 4. Thus the will is disposed to fall in with those things which, in its depraved state, it could never be reconciled to.

Particularly, 1. The soul is reconciled to the covenant of peace. The Lord God proposes a covenant of peace to sinners, a covenant which he himself has framed, and registered in the Bible : but they are not pleased with it. Nay, unregenerate hearts cannot be pleased with it. Were it put into their hands to frame it according to their minds, they would blot many things out of it which God has put in, and put in many things which God has kept out. But the renewed heart is entirely satisfied with the covenant, 2 Sam. xxiii. 5, " He hath made with me an everlasting covenant, ordered in all things and sure ; this is all my salvation, and all my desire." Though the covenant could not be brought down to their depraved will, their will is, by grace, brought up to the covenant : they are well pleased with it ; there is nothing in it which they would have out ; nor is any thing left out of it, which they would have in.—2. The will is disposed to receive Christ Jesus the Lord. The soul is content to submit to him. Regenerating grace undermines, and brings down the towering imaginations of the heart, raised up against its rightful Lord; it breaks the iron sinew, which kept the sinner from bowing to him ; and disposes him to be no more stiff-necked, but to yield. He is willing to have on the yoke of Christ's commands, to take up the cross, and to follow him. He is content to take Christ on any terms, Psalm cx. 3, " Thy people shall be willing in the day of thy power."

The mind being savingly enlightened, and the will renewed, the sinner is thereby determined and enabled to answer the gospel call So the chief work in regeneration is done; the fort of the heart is taken; there is room made for the Lord Jesus Christ in the inmost parts of the soul; the inner door of the will being now opened to him, as well as the outer door of the understanding. In one word, Christ is passively received into the heart; he is come into the soul, by his quickening Spirit, whereby spiritual life is given to the man, who in himself was dead in sin. His first vital act we may conceive to be an active receiving of Jesus Christ, discerned in his glorious excellencies; that is a believing on him, a closing with him, as discerned, offered and exhibited in the word of his grace, the glorious Gospel: the immediate effect of which is union with him, John i. 12, 13, "To as many as received him to them gave he power," or privilege, "to become the sons of God, even to them that believe on his name: which were born not of blood, nor of the will of the flesh, nor of the will of man, but of God." Eph. iii. 17, "That Christ may dwell in your hearts by faith." Christ having taken the heart by storm, and triumphantly entered into it, in regeneration, the soul by faith yields itself to him, as it is expressed, 2 Chron. xxx. 8. Thus, this glorious King who came into the heart, by his Spirit, dwells in it by faith. The soul being drawn runs; and being effectually called, comes.

3. In regeneration there is a happy change made on the affections; they are both rectified and regulated.

(1.) This change rectifies the affections, placing them on suitable objects. 2 Thess. iii. 5, "The Lord direct your hearts into the love of God." The regenerate man's desires are rectified; they are set on God himself, and the things above. He, who before cried with the world, "Who will shew us any good?" has changed his note, and says, "Lord, lift up the light of thy countenance upon us,'" Psalm iv. 6. Before, he saw no beauty in Christ, for which he was to be desired; but now he is all he desires, he is altogether lovely, Cant. v. 16. The main stream of his desires is turned to run towards God; for there is the one thing he desires, Psalm xxvii. 4. He desires to be holy as well as happy; and rather to be gracious than great. His hopes, which before were low, and fastened down to things on earth, are now raised, and set on the glory which is to be revealed. He entertains the hope of eternal life, founded on the word of promise, Tit. i. 2. Which hope he has, as an anchor of the soul, fixing the heart under trials, Heb vi. 19. It puts him upon purifying himself, even as God is pure 1 John iii. 3. For he is begotten again unto a lively hope, 1 Pet. i. 3. His love is raised, and set on God himself, Psalm xviii. 1; on his holy law, Psalm cxix. 97. Though it strike against his most beloved lust, he says, "The law is holy, and the commandment holy, and just, and good," Rom. viii. 12. He loves the ordinances of God," Psalm lxxxiv. 1, "How amiable are thy tabernacles, O Lord of hosts!" Being passed from death unto life, he loves the brethren, 1 John iii. 14; the people of God, as they are called, 1 Pet. ii. 10. He loves God for himself; and what is God's, for his sake. Yea, as being a child of God, he loves his own enemies.—His heavenly Father is compassionate and benevolent: "He maketh his sun to rise on the evil and on the good; and sendeth rain on the just and on the unjust:" therefore he is in like manner disposed, Matt. v. 44, 45. His hatred is turned against sin, in himself and others, Psalm ci. 3, "I hate the work of them that turn aside, it shall not cleave to me." He groans under the body of it, and longs for deliverance, Rom. vii. 24, "O wretched man that I am! who shall deliver me from the body of this death?" His joys and delights are in God the Lord, in the light of his countenance, in his law, and in his people, because they are like him. Sin is what he chiefly fears: it is a fountain of sorrow to him now, though formerly a spring of pleasure.

(2.) It regulates the affections placed on suitable objects. Our affections, when placed on the creature, are naturally exhorbitant: when we joy in it, we are apt to overjoy; and when we sorrow, we are ready to sorrow overmuch: but grace bridles these affections, clips their wings, and keeps them within bounds, that they overflow not all their banks. It makes a man "hate his father, and mother, and wife, and children; yea, and his own life also," comparatively; that is, to love them less than he loves God, Luke xiv. 26. It also rectifies lawful affections; bringing them forth from right principles, and directing them to right ends. There may be unholy desires after Christ and his grace; as when men desire Christ, not from any love to him, but merely out of love to themselves. "Give us of your oil," said the foolish virgins, "for our lamps are gone out," Matt. xxv. 8. There may be an unsanctified sorrow for sin; as when one sorrows for it, not because it is displeasing to God, but only because of the wrath annexed to it, as did Pharaoh, Judas, and others. So a man may love his father and mother from mere natural principles, without any respect to the command of God binding him thereto. But grace sanctifies the affections, in such cases, making them to run in a new channel of love to God, respect to his commands, and regard to his glory. Again, grace raises the affections where they are too low. It gives the chief seat in them to God, and pulls down all other rivals, whether persons or things, making them lie at his feet. Psalm lxxiii. 25, "Whom have I in heaven but thee? and there is none upon earth that I desire besides thee." He is loved for himself, and other persons or things for his sake. What is lovely in them, to the renewed heart, is some ray of the divine goodness appearing in them: for unto gracious souls they shine only by borrowed light. This accounts for the saints loving all men; and yet hating those that hate God, and contemning the wicked as vile persons. They hate and contemn them for their wickedness; there is nothing of God in that, and therefore nothing lovely nor honourable in it: but they love them for their commendable qualities or perfections, whether natural or moral; because, in whomsoever these are, they are from God, and can be traced to him as their fountain.

Finally, regenerating grace sets the affections so firmly on God, that the man is disposed, at God's command, to quit his hold of every thing else, in order to keep his hold of Christ; to hate father and mother, in comparison with Christ, Luke xiv. 26. It makes even lawful enjoyments, like Joseph's mantle to hang loose about a man, that he may quit them, when he is in danger of being ensnared by holding them.

If the stream of our affections were never turned, we are, doubtless, going down the stream into the pit. If "the lust of the eye, the lust of the flesh, and the pride of life," have the throne in our hearts, which should be possessed by the Father, Son, and Holy Ghost; if we never had so much love to God, as to ourselves; if sin has been somewhat bitter to us, but never so bitter as suffering, never so bitter as the pain of being weaned from it; truly we are strangers to this saving change.—For grace turns the affections upside down, whenever it comes into the heart.

4. The conscience is renewed. As a new light is set up in the soul, in regeneration, conscience is enlightened, instructed and informed. That candle of the Lord, Prov. xx. 27, is now snuffed and brightened; so that it shines, and sends forth its light into the most retired corners of the heart; discovering sins which the soul was not aware of before: and, in a special manner, discovering the corruption or depravity of nature, that seed and spawn whence all actual sins proceed. This produces the new complaint, Rom. vii. 24, "O wretched man that I am! who shall deliver me from the body of this death?" Conscience, which lay sleeping in the man's bosom before, is now awakened, and makes its voice to be heard through the whole soul; therefore there is no more rest for him in the sluggard's bed; he must get up and be doing, arise, "haste, and escape for his life." It powerfully incites to obedience, even

in the most spiritual acts, which lie not within the view of the natural conscience; and powerfully restrains from sin, even from those sins which do not lie open to the observation of the world. It urges the sovereign authority of God, to which the heart is now reconciled, and which it willingly acknowledges: and so it engages the man to his duty, whatever be the hazard from the world; for it fills the heart so with the fear of God, that the force of the fear of man is broken. This has engaged many to put their life in their hand, and follow the cause of religion, which they once contemned, and resolutely walk in the path they formerly abhorred, Gal. i. 23, "He which persecuted us in times past, now preacheth the faith which once he destroyed." Guilt now makes the conscience smart. It has bitter remorse for sins past, which fills the soul with anxiety, sorrow, and self-loathing. And every new reflection on these sins is apt to affect, and make its wounds bleed afresh with regret. It is made tender, in point of sin and duty, for the time to come: being once burnt, it dreads the fire, and fears to break the hedge where it was formerly bit by the serpent. Finally, the renewed conscience drives the sinner to Jesus Christ, as the only Physician who can draw out the sting of guilt; and whose blood alone can purge the conscience from dead works, Heb. ix. 14, refusing all ease offered to it from any other hand. This is an evidence that the conscience is not only fired, as it may be in an unregenerate state, but oiled also, with regenerating grace.

5. As the memory wanted not its share of depravity, it is also bettered by regenerating grace. The memory is weakened, with respect to those things that are not worth their room therein; and men are taught to forget injuries, and drop their resentments, Matt. v. 44, 45, "Do good to them that hate you, and pray for them which despitefully use you—that ye may be," that is, appear to be, "the children of your Father which is in heaven." It is strengthened for spiritual things. We have Solomon's receipt for an ill memory, Prov. iii. 1, "My son," saith he, "forget not my law." But how shall it be kept in mind? "Let thine heart keep my commandments." Grace makes a heart-memory, even where there is no good head-memory, Psalm cxix. 11, "Thy word have I hid in mine heart." The heart, truly touched with the powerful sweetness of truth, will help the memory to retain what is so relished. If divine truths made deeper impressions on our hearts, they would impress themselves with more force on our memories, Psalm cxix. 93, "I will never forget thy precepts, for with them thou hast quickened me." Grace sanctifies the memory. Many have large, but unsanctified memories, which serve only to gather knowledge, whereby to aggravate their condem-

nation; but the renewed memory serves to "remember his commandments to do them," Psalm ciii. 18. It is a sacred storehouse, from whence a Christian is furnished in his way to Zion; for faith and hope are often supplied out of it, in a dark hour. It is the storehouse of former experiences; and these are the believer's way-marks, by noticing of which he comes to know where he is, even in a dark time. Psalm xlii. 6, "O my God, my soul is cast down within me: therefore will I remember thee from the land of Jordan," &c. It also helps the soul to godly sorrow and self-loathing, presenting old guilt anew before the conscience, and making it bleed afresh, though the sin be already pardoned; Psalm xxv. 7, "Remember not the sins of my youth." Where unpardoned guilt is lying on the sleeping conscience, it is often employed to bring in a word, which in a moment sets the whole soul on the stir; as when "Peter remembered the words of Jesus—he went out and wept bitterly," Matt. xxvi. 75. The word of God laid up in a sanctified memory, serves a man to resist temptations, puts the sword in his hand against his spiritual enemies, and is a light to direct his steps in the way of religion and righteousness.

6. There is a change made on the body, and the members thereof, in respect of their use; they are consecrated to the Lord. Even "the body is—for the Lord," 1 Cor. vi. 13. It is "the temple of the Holy Ghost," ver. 19. The members thereof, that were formerly "instruments of unrighteousness unto sin," become "instruments of righteousness unto God," Rom. vi. 13, "servants to righteousness unto holiness," ver. 19. The eye, that conveyed sinful imaginations into the heart, is under a covenant, Job xxxi. 1, to do so no more; but to serve the soul, in viewing the works, and reading the word, of God. The ear, that had often been death's porter, to let in sin, is turned to be the gate of life, by which the word of life enters the soul. The tongue, that set on fire the whole course of nature, is restored to the office it was designed for by the Creator; namely, to be an instrument of glorifying him, and setting forth his praise. In a word, the whole man is for God, in soul and body, which by this blessed change are made his.

7. This gracious change shines forth in the conversation. Even the outward man is renewed. A new heart makes newness of life. When "the king's daughter is all glorious within, her clothing is of wrought gold," Psalm xlv. 13. "The single eye" makes "the whole body full of light," Matt. vi. 22. This change will appear in every part of a man's conversation; particularly in the following things.

(1.) In the change of his company. Formerly, he despised the company of the saints, but now they are "the excellent, in whom is all his delight," Psalm xvi. 3. "I am a companion of all that fear thee, saith the royal psalmist, Psalm cxix. 63. A renewed man joins himself with the saints; for he and they are like-minded, in that which is their main work and business; they have all one new nature: they are travelling to Immanuel's land, and converse together in the language of Canaan. In vain do men pretend to religion, while ungodly company is their choice; for " a companion of fools shall be destroyed," Prov. xiii. 20. Religion will make a man shy of throwing himself into an ungodly family, or any unnecessary familiarity with wicked men; as one who is healthy will beware of going into an infected house.

(2.) In his relative capacity, he will be a new man. Grace makes men gracious in their several relations, and naturally leads them to the conscientious performance of relative duties. It does not only make good men and good women, but makes good subjects, good husbands, good wives, children, servants, and, in a word, good relatives in the church, commonwealth, and family. It is a just exception made against the religion of many, namely that they are bad relatives, they are ill husbands, wives, masters, servants, &c. How can we prove ourselves to be new creatures, if we be just such as we were before, in our several relations? 2 Cor. v. 17, "Therefore, if any man be in Christ, he is a new creature: old things are past away; behold, all things are become new." Real godliness will gain a testimony to a man, from the consciences of his nearest relations; though they know more of his sinful infirmities than others do, as we see in the case, 2 Kings iv. 1, "Thy servant my husband is dead, and thou knowest that thy servant did fear the Lord."

(3.) In the way of his following his wordly business, there is a great change. It appears to be no more his all, as it was before. Though saints apply themselves to worldly business, as well as others, yet their hearts are not swallowed up in it. It is evident that they are carrying on a trade with heaven, as well as a trade with earth, Phil. iii. 20, "For our conversation is in heaven," They go about their employment in the world, as a duty laid upon them by the Lord of all, doing their lawful business as the will of God, Eph. vi. 7, working, because he has said, "Thou shalt not steal."

(4.) Such have a special concern for the advancement of the kingdom of Christ in the world: they espouse the interests of religion, and "prefer Jerusalem above their chief joy," Psalm cxxxvii. 6. How privately soever they live, grace gives them a public spirit, will concern itself in the ark and work of God, in the Gospel of God, and in the people of God, even in those of them whom they never saw. As children of God, they naturally care for these things. They have a new concern for the spiritual good of others : no sooner do they taste of the power of grace themselves, but they are inclined to set up to be agents for Christ and holiness in the world; as appears in the case of the woman of Samaria, who when Christ had manifested himself to her, "went her way into the city, and said unto the men, Come, see a man which told me all things that ever I did: is not this the Christ?" John iv. 28, 29. They have seen and felt the evil of sin, and therefore pity the world lying in wickedness. They would fain pluck the brands out of the fire, remembering that they themselves were plucked out of it. They labour to commend religion to others, both by word and example; and rather deny themselves the liberty in indifferent things, than, by the uncharitable use of it, destroy others; 1 Cor viii. 13, "Wherefore, if meat make my brother to offend, I will eat no flesh while the world standeth, lest I make my brother to offend."

(5.) In their use of lawful comforts, there is a great change. They rest not in them, as their end; but use them as means to help them in their way. They draw their satisfaction from the higher springs even while lower springs are running. Thus Hannah having obtained a son, rejoiced not so much in the gift, as in the giver, 1 Sam. ii. 1, "And Hannah prayed and said, My heart rejoiceth in the Lord." Yea, when the comforts of life are gone, they can subsist without them, and "rejoice in the Lord although the fig-tree do not blossom," Hab. iii. 17, 18. Grace teaches to use the conveniences of the present life as pilgrims; and to shew a holy moderation in all things. The heart, which formally revelled in these things without fear, is now shy of being over much pleased with them. Being apprehensive of danger, it uses them warily; as the dogs of Egypt run, while they lap their water out of the river Nile, for fear of the crocodiles that are in it.

(6.) This change shines forth in the man's performance of religious duties. He who lived in the neglect of them will do so no more, if once the grace of God enter into his heart. If a man be new-born, he will desire the sincere milk of the word, 1 Pet. ii. 2, 3. Whenever the prayerless person gets the Spirit of grace, he will be in him a Spirit of supplication, Zech. xii. 10. It is as natural for one that is born again to pray, as for the new-born babe to cry. Acts ix. 11, "Behold, he prayeth!" His heart will be a temple for God, and his house a church. His devotion, which before was superficial and formal, is now spiritual and lively; for as much as heart and tongue are touched with a live coal from heaven: and he rests not in the mere performance of duties, as careful only to get his task done, but in every duty seeks communion with God in Christ: justly considering them as means appointed of God for that end, and reckoning himself disappointed if he miss of it. Thus far of the nature of regeneration.

II. I come to shew why this change is called regeneration a being born again. It is so called, because of the resemblance between natural and spiritual generation, which lies in the following particulars.

1. Natural generation is a mysterious thing: and so is spiritual generation, John iii. 8, "The wind bloweth where it listeth, and thou hearest the sound thereof, but canst not tell whence it cometh and whither it goeth: so is every one that is born of the Spirit." The work of the Spirit is felt; but his way of working is a mystery we cannot comprehend. A new light is let into the mind, and the will is renewed; but how that light is conveyed thither, how the will is fettered with cords of love, and how the rebel is made a willing captive, we can no more tell, than we can tell "how the bones do grow in the womb of her that is with child," Eccl. xi. 5. As a man hears the sound of the wind, and finds it stirring, but knows not where it begins, and where it ends; "so is every one that is born of the Spirit:" he finds the change that is made upon him; but how it is produced he knoweth not. One thing he may know that whereas he was blind, now he seeth: but "the seed of grace" "springs and grows up, he knoweth not how," Mark iv. 26, 27.

2. In both, the creature comes to a being it had not before. The child is not, till it be generate; and a man has no gracious being, no being in grace, till he is regenerate. Regeneration is not so much the curing of a sick man, as "the quickening of a dead man," Eph. ii. 1—5. Man in his depraved state, is a mere nonentity in grace, and is brought into a new being by the power of Him "who calleth things that be not as though they were;" being "created in Jesus Christ unto good works," Eph. ii. 10. Therefore our Lord Jesus, to give ground of hope to the Laodiceans, in their wretched and miserable state, proposes himself as "the beginning of the creation of God," Rev. iii. 14, namely, the active beginning of it; "for all things were made by him" at first, John i. 3. From whence they might gather, that as he made them when they were nothing, he could make them over again, when worse than nothing; the same hand that made them his creatures, could make them new creatures.

As the child is passive in generation, so is the child of God in regeneration. The one contributes nothing to its own generation; neither does the other contribute any thing, by way of efficiency, to its own regeneration: for though a man may lay himself down at the pool, yet he hath no hand in moving the water, no power in performing the cure. One is born the child of a king, another the child of a beggar: the child has no hand at all in this difference. God leaves some in their depraved state; others he brings into a state of grace, or regeneracy. If thou be thus honoured, no thanks to thee; for "who maketh thee to differ from another? and what hast thou that thou didst not receive?" 1 Cor. iv. 7.

4. There is a wonderful contexture of parts in both births. Admirable is the structure of man's body, in which there is such a variety of organs; nothing wanting, nothing superfluous. The psalmist, considering his own body, looks on it as a piece of marvellous work; "I am fearfully and wonderfully made," saith he, Psalm cxxxix. 14, "and curiously wrought in the lower parts of the earth," ver. 15; that is, in the womb, where I know not how the bones grow, any more than I know what is doing in the lowest parts of the earth. In natural generation we are curiously wrought, like a piece of needle-work; as the word imports: even so it is in regeneration: Psalm xlv. 14, "She shall be brought unto the King in raiment of needle-work," raiment curiously wrought. It is the same word in both texts. What that raiment is, the apostle tells us, Eph. iv. 24. It is "the new man, which after God is created in righteousness and true holiness." This is the raiment which he saith, in the same place, we must put on; not excluding the imputed righteousness of Christ. Both are curiously wrought, as masterpieces of the manifold wisdom of God. O the wonderful contexture of graces in the new creature! O glorious creature, new-made after the image of God! It is grace for grace in Christ, which makes up this new man, John i. 16; even as in bodily generation, the child has member for member in the parent; has every member which the parent has in a certain proportion.

5. All this, in both cases, has its rise from that which is in itself very small and inconsiderable. O the power of God, in making such a creature of the corruptible seed, and much more in bringing forth the new creature from such small beginnings! It is as "the little cloud, like a man's hand," which spread, till "heaven was black with clouds and wind, and there was a great rain," 1 Kings xviii. 44, 45. A man gets a word at a sermon, which hundreds besides him hear, and let slip: but it remains with him, works in him, and never leaves him, till the little world is turned upside down by it; that is, till he becomes a new man. It is like the vapour that

got up into Ahasuerus's head, and cut off sleep from his eyes, Esth. vi. 1, which proved a spring of such motions as never ceased, until Mordecai, in royal pomp, was brought on horseback through the streets, proud Haman trudging at his foot; the same Haman afterwards hanged, Mordecai advanced, and the church delivered from Haman's hellish plot. "The grain of mustard seed becometh a tree," Mat. xiii. 31, 32. God loves to bring great things out of small beginnings.

6. Natural generation is carried on by degrees. Job x. 10, "Hast thou not poured me out as milk, and curdled me like cheese?" So is regeneration. It is with the soul, ordinarily, in regeneration, as with the blind man cured by our Lord, who first "saw men as trees walking," afterward "saw every man clearly," Mark viii. 23—25. It is true, regeneration being, strictly speaking, a passage from death to life, the soul is quickened in a moment; like as when the embryo is brought to perfection in the womb, the soul is infused into the lifeless lump. Nevertheless, we may imagine somewhat like conception in spiritual regeneration, whereby the soul is prepared for quickening; and the new creature is capable of growth, 1 Peter ii. 2, and of having life more abundantly, John x. 10.

7. In both there are new relations. The regenerate may call God, Father; for they are his children, John i. 12, 13, "begotten of him," 1 Pet. i. 3. The bride, the Lamb's wife, that is, the church, is their mother, Gal. iv. 26. They are related, as brethren and sisters, to angels and glorified saints; "the family of heaven." They are of the heavenly stock: the meanest of them, "the base things of the world," 1 Cor. i. 28, the kinless things, as the word imports, who cannot boast of the blood that runs in their veins, are yet, by their new birth, near of kin with the excellent in the earth.

8. There is a likeness between the parent and the child. Every thing that generates, generates its like; and the regenerate are "partakers of the divine nature," 2 Peter i. 4. The moral perfections of the divine nature are, in measure and degree, communicated to the renewed soul: thus the divine image is restored; so that, as the child resembles the father, the new creature resembles God himself, being holy as he is holy.

9. As there is no birth without pain, both to the mother and to the child, so there is great pain in bringing forth the new creature. The children have more or less of these birth-pains, whereby they are "pricked in their heart," Acts ii. 37. The soul has sore pains when under conviction and humiliation. "A wounded spirit who can bear?" The mother is pained; "Zion travails," Isaiah lxvi. 8.

She sighs, groans, cries, and has hard labour, in her ministers and members, to bring forth children to her Lord, Gal. iv. 19, "My little children, of whom I travail in birth again, until Christ be formed in you." Never was a mother more feelingly touched with "joy, that a man child is born into the world," than she is upon the new birth of her children. But, what is more remarkable than all this, we read not only of our Lord Jesus Christ's "travail," or toil "of soul," Isaiah liii. 11, but, what is more directly to our purpose, of his "pains," or pangs, as of one travailing in childbirth; so the word used, Acts ii. 24, properly signifies. Well might he call the new creature, as Rachel called her dear-bought son, Benoni, that is, the son of my sorrow; and as she called another, Naphtali, that is, my wrestling: for the pangs of that travail put him to "strong crying and tears," Heb. v. 7; yea, into an "agony and bloody sweat," Luke xxii. 44. And in the end he died of these pangs; they became to him "the pains of death," Acts ii. 24.

I shall now apply this doctrine.

USE I. By what is said, you may try whether you are in the state of grace or not. If you are brought out of the state of wrath or ruin, into the state of grace or salvation, you are new creatures, you are born again. But you will say, How shall we know whether we are born again, or not? *Answer.* Were you to ask me, if the sun were risen, and how you should know whether it were risen or not? I would bid you look up to the heavens, and see it with your eyes. And, would you know if the light be risen in your heart? Look in, and see. Grace is light, and discovers itself. Look into thy mind, see if it has been illuminated in the knowledge of God. Hast thou been inwardly taught what God is? Were thine eyes ever turned inward to see thyself; the sinfulness of thy depraved state, the corruption of thy nature; the sins of thy heart and life? Wast thou ever led into a view of the exceeding sinfulness of sin? Have thine eyes seen King Jesus in his beauty; the manifold wisdom of God in him, his transcendent excellence, and absolute fulness and sufficiency, with the vanity and emptiness of all things else? Next, What change is there on thy will? Are the fetters taken off, wherewith it was formerly bound up from moving heavenward? Has thy will got a new turn? Dost thou find an aversion to sin, and an inclination to good, wrought in thy heart? Is thy soul turned towards God, as thy chief end? Is thy will new-moulded into some measure of conformity to the preceptive and providential will of God? Art thou heartily reconciled to the covenant of peace, and fixedly disposed to the receiving of Christ, as he is offered in the gospel? And as to a change on your affections, are they rectified, and placed on right objects? Are your desires going out after God? Are they to his name, and the remembrance of him? Isaiah xxvi. 8. Are your hopes in him? Is your love set upon him, and your hatred set against sin? Does your offending a good God affect your heart with sorrow, and do you fear sin more than suffering? Are your affections regulated? Are they, with respect to created comforts, brought down, as being too high; and with respect to God in Christ, raised up, as being too low? Has he the chief seat in your heart? And are all your lawful worldly comforts and enjoyments laid at his feet? Has thy conscience been enlightened and awakened, refusing all ease, but from the application of the blood of a Redeemer? Is thy memory sanctified, thy body consecrated to the service of God? And art thou now walking in newness of life? Thus you may discover whether you are born again or not.

But, for your farther help in this matter, I will discourse a little of another sign of regeneration, namely, the love of the brethren; an evidence whereby the weakest and most timorous saints have often had comfort, when they could have little or no consolation from other marks proposed to them. This the apostle lays down, 1 John iii. 14, "We know that we have passed from death unto life, because we love the brethren." It is not to be thought that the apostle, by the brethren in this place means brethren by a common relation to the first Adam, but to the second Adam, Christ Jesus; because, however true it is, that universal benevolence, a good will to the whole race of mankind, takes place in the renewed soul, as being a lively lineament of the divine image, yet the whole context speaks of those that are "the sons of God," ver. 1, 2; "children of of God," ver. 10; "born of God," ver. 9; distinguishing between "the children of God," and "the children of the devil," ver. 10; between those that are "of the devil," ver. 8, 12, and those that are "of God," ver. 10. The text itself comes in as a reason why we should not marvel that the world hates the brethren, the children of God, ver. 13. How can we marvel at it, seeing the love of the brethren is an evidence of one's having passed from death to life? Therefore it were absurd to look for that love amongst the men of the world, who are dead in trespasses and sins. They cannot love the brethren; no wonder, then, that they hate them. Wherefore it is plain, that by brethren here, are meant brethren by regeneration.

Now, in order to set this mark of regeneration in a true light, consider these three things. 1. This love to the brethren, is a love to them as such. Then do we love them in the sense of the text, when the grace, or image of God in them, is the chief motive of our love to them. When we love the godly for their godliness, the saints for their sanctity or holiness, then we love God in them, and so may conclude were born of God; for "every one that loveth Him that begat, loveth him also that is begotten of him," 1 John v. 1. Hypocrites may love saints, on account of civil relations to them; because of their obliging conversation; for their being of the same opinion as to outward religious matters; and on many other such like accounts, whereby wicked men may be induced to love the godly. But happy they who love them merely for grace in them; for their heaven-born temper and disposition; who can pick this pearl even out of infirmities in and about them; lay hold of it, and love them for it. 2. It is a love that will be given to all in whom the grace of God appears. They that love one saint, because he is a saint, will have "love to all the saints," Eph. i. 15. They will love all, who, in their view, bear the image of God. Those that cannot love a gracious person in rags, but confine their love to those of them who wear gay clothing, have not this love to the brethren in them. Those who confine their love to a party, to whom God has not confined his grace, are souls too narrow to be put among the children. In what points soever men differ from us, in their judgment or way; yet if they appear to agree with us, in love to God, and our Saviour Jesus Christ, and in bearing his image, we shall love them as brethren, if we are of the heavenly family. 3. If this love be in us, the more grace any person appears to be possessed of, he will be the more beloved by us. The more vehemently the holy fire of grace doth flame in any, the hearts of true Christians will be the more warmed in love to them.—It is not with th~~ ~~ints as with many other men, who make themselves the standards for others; and love them so far as they think they are like themselves. But, if they seem to outshine and darken them, their love is turned to hatred and envy, and they endeavour to detract from the due praise of their exemplary piety; because nothing relisheth with them, in the practice of religion, that goes beyond their own measure; what of the life and power of religion appears in others, serves only to raise the serpentine grudge in their pharisaical hearts. But as for those who are born again, their love and affection to the brethren bears proportion to the degrees of the divine image they discern in them.

Now, if you would improve these to the knowledge of your state, I would advise you, 1. To set apart some time, when you are at home, for a review of your case, to try your state by what has been said. Many have comfort and clearness as to their state, at a ser-

men, who in a little time lose it again; because while they hear the word preached, they make application of it; but do not consider these things more deliberately and leisurely when alone. The impression is too sudden and short to give lasting comfort; and it is often so inconsiderate, that it has bad consequences. Therefore set about this work at home, after earnest and serious prayer to God for his help in it. Complain not of your want of time while the night follows the busy day; nor of place, while fields and outhouses are to be got. 2. Renew your repentance before the Lord. Guilt lying on the conscience, unrepented of, may darken all your evidences and marks of grace. It provokes the Spirit of grace to withdraw; and when he goes, our light ceases. It is not a fit time for a saint to read his evidences, when the candle is blown out by some conscience-wounding guilt. 3. Exert the powers of the new nature; let the graces of the divine Spirit discover themselves in you by action. If you would know whether there is sacred fire in your breast, or not, you must blow the coal; for although it exist, and be a live coal, yet if it be under the ashes, it will give you no light. Settle in your hearts a firm purpose, through the grace that is in Christ Jesus, to comply with every known duty, and watch against every known sin, having readiness of mind to be instructed in what you know not. If gracious souls would thus manage their inquiries into their state, it is likely that they would have a comfortable issue. And if others would take such a solemn review, and make trial of their state, impartially examining themselves before the tribunal of their consciences, they might have a timely discovery of their own sinfulness; but the neglect of self-examination leaves most men under sad delusions as to their state, and deprives many saints of the comfortable sight of the grace of God in them.

But that I may afford some farther help to true Christians in their inquiries into their state, I shall propose and briefly answer some cases or doubts, which may possibly hinder some persons from the comfortable view of their happy state. The children's bread must not be withheld; though, while it is held forth to them, the dogs should snatch at it.

Case 1. "I doubt if I be regenerate, because I know not the precise time of my conversion; nor can I trace the particular steps of the way in which it was brought to pass." *Answer.* Though it is very desirable to be able to give an account of the beginning, and the gradual advances, of the Lord's work upon our souls, as some saints can distinctly do, the manner of the Spirit's working being still a mystery, yet this is not necessary to prove the truth of grace.

Happy he that can say, in this case, as the blind man in the Gospel, "One thing I know, that whereas I was blind, now I see. As, when we see flame, we know there is fire, though we know not how or when it began; so the truth of grace may be discerned in us, though we know not how or when it was dropped into our hearts. If thou canst perceive the happy change which is wrought on thy soul; if thou findest thy mind is enlightened, thy will inclined to comply with the will of God in all things; especially to fall in with the divine plan of salvation, through a crucified Redeemer; in vain dost thou trouble thyself, and refuse comfort, because thou knowest not how and what way it was brought about.

CASE 2. "If I were a new creature, sin could not prevail against me as it doth." *Answer.* Though we must not lay pillows for hypocrites to rest their heads upon, who indulge themselves in their sins, and make the doctrine of God's grace subservient to their lusts, lying down contentedly in the bond of iniquity like men that are fond of golden chains; yet it must be owned, "the just man falleth seven times a-day; and iniquity may prevail against the children of God. But if thou art groaning under the weight of the body of death, the corruption of thy nature; loathing thyself for the sins of thy heart and life; striving to mortify thy lusts; fleeing daily to the blood of Christ for pardon; and looking to his spirit for sanctification: though thou mayest be obliged to say with the Psalmist, "Iniquities prevail against me;" yet thou mayest add with him, "As for our transgressions thou shalt purge them away, Psal. lxv. 3. The new creature does not yet possess the house alone: it dwells by the side of an ill neighbour, namely, remaining corruption, the relics of depraved nature. They struggle together for the mastery: "The flesh lusteth against the spirit, and the spirit against the flesh," Gal. v. 17. And sometimes corruption prevails, bringing the child of God into captivity to the law of sin, Rom. vii. 23. Let not therefore the prevailing of corruption make thee, in this case, conclude thou art none of God's children: but let it humble thee, to be the more watchful, and to thirst the more intensely after Jesus Christ, his blood and Spirit; and that very disposition will evidence a principle of grace in thee, which seeks the destruction of sin that prevails so often against thee.

CASE 3. "I find the motions of sin in my heart more violent since the Lord began his work on my soul, than they were before that time. Can this consist with a change of my nature?" *Answer.* Dreadful is the case of many, who, after God has had a remarkable dealing with their souls, tending to their reformation, have thrown off all bonds, and have become grossly and openly immoral and profane; as if the devil had returned into their hearts with seven spirits worse than himself. All I shall say to such persons is, that their state is exceedingly dangerous; they are in danger of sinning against the Holy Ghost, therefore let them repent, before it be too late. But if it be not thus with you; though corruption is stirring itself more violently than formerly, as if all the forces of hell were raised, to hold fast, or bring back, a fugitive; yet these stirrings may consist with a change of your nature. When the restraint of grace is newly laid upon corruption, it is no wonder if it acts more vigorously than before, "warring against the law of the mind," Rom. vii. 23. The motions of sin may really be most violent, when the new principle is brought in to cast it out. The sun sending its beams through the window, discovers the motes in the house, and their motions, which were not seen before; so the light of grace may discover the risings and actings of corruption, in another manner than ever the man saw them before, though they really do not rise nor act more vigorously. Sin is not quite dead in the regenerate soul; it is but dying, and dying a lingering death, being crucified; no wonder there are great fightings, when it is sick at the heart, and death is at the door. Besides, temptations may be more in number, and stronger, while Satan is striving to bring you back, who are escaped, than while he only endeavoured to retain you: "After ye were illuminated, ye endured a great fight of affliction," says the apostle to the Hebrews, chap. x. 32. But "cast not away your confidence," ver. 35. Remember his "grace is sufficient for you, and the God of peace shall bruise Satan under your feet shortly." Pharaoh and his Egyptians never made such a formidable appearance against the Israelites, as at the Red Sea, after they were brought out of Egypt: but then were the pursuers nearest to a total overthrow, Exod. chap. xiv. Let not this case, therefore, make you raze the foundations of your trust; but be ye emptied of self, and strong in the Lord, and in the power of his might, and you shall come off victorious.

CASE 4. "But when I compare my love to God with my love to some created enjoyments, I find the pulse of my affections beat stronger to the creature than to the Creator. How then can I call him Father? Nay, alas! those turnings of heart within me, and glowings of affection to him, which I had, are gone; so that I fear all the love which I ever had to the Lord has been but a fit and flash of affection, such as hypocrites often have. *Answer.* It cannot be denied, that the predominant love of the world is a certain mark of an unregenerate state, 1 John ii. 15, "If any man love the world, the love of the Father is not in him." Nevertheless, those are not always the strongest affections which are most violent. A man's affections may be more moved, on some occasions, by an object that is little regarded, than by another that is exceedingly beloved; even as a little brook sometimes makes more noise than a great river. The strength of our affections is to be measured by the firmness and fixedness of the root, not by the violence of their actings. Suppose a person meeting with a friend, who has been long abroad, finds his affections more vehemently acting towards his friend on that occasion, than towards his own wife and children; will he therefore say, that he loves his friend more than them? Surely not. Even so, although the Christian may find himself more moved in his love to the creature, than in his love to God; yet it is not therefore to be said, that he loves the creature more than God, seeing love to God is always more firmly rooted in a gracious heart, than love to any created enjoyment whatever; as appears when competition arises in such a manner, that the one or other is to be foregone. Would you then know your case? Retire into your own hearts, and there lay the two in the balance, and try which of them weighs down the other. Ask thyself, as in the sight of God, whether thou wouldst part with Christ for the creature, or part with the creature for Christ, if thou wert left to thy choice in the matter? If you find your heart disposed to part with what is dearest to you in the world for Christ at his call, you have no reason to conclude you love the creature more than God; but, on the contrary, that you love God more than the creature, although you do not feel such violent motions in the love of God, as in the love of some created thing, Matt. x. 37, "He that loveth father or mother more than me, is not worthy of me." Luke xiv. 26, "If any man come to me, and hate not his father and mother—he cannot be my disciple." From which texts compared we may infer, that he who hates, that is, is ready to part with, father and mother for Christ, is, in our Lord's account, one that loves them less than him, and not one who loves father and mother more than him. Moreover, you are to consider that there is a twofold love to Christ. 1. There is a sensible love to him, which is felt as a dart in the heart, and makes a holy love-sickness in the soul, arising from want of enjoyment, as in that case of the spouse, Cant. v. 8, "I charge you, O daughters of Jerusalem, if ye find my beloved, that ye tell him that I am sick of love:" or else from the fulness of it, as in Cant. ii. 5, "Stay me with flagons, comfort me with apples; for I am sick of love." These glowings of affection are usually wrought in young converts, who are ordinarily made "to sing in the days of their youth," Hos. ii. 15. While the fire-edge is upon the young convert, he looks upon others, reputed to be godly, and not finding them in such a temper or disposition as himself, he is ready to censure them; and to think there is far less religion in the world than indeed there is. But when his own cup comes to settle below the brim, and he finds that in himself which made him question the state of others, he is more humbled, and feels more and more the necessity of daily recourse to the blood of Christ for pardon, and to the Spirit of Christ for sanctification; and thus grows downwards in humiliation, self-loathing, and self-denial. 2. There is a rational love to Christ, which, without these sensible emotions felt in the former case, evidences itself by a dutiful regard to the divine authority and command. When one bears such a love to Christ, though the vehement strings of affection be wanting, yet he is truly tender of offending a gracious God; endeavours to walk before him unto all well pleasing; and is grieved at the heart for what is displeasing unto him, 1 John v. 3, "For this is the love of God, that we keep his commandments." Now, although that sensible love does not always continue with you, you have no reason to deem it a hypocritical fit, while the rational love remains with you; any more than a loving and faithful wife needs question her love to her husband, when her fondness is abated.

CASE 5. "The attainments of hypocrites and apostates are a terror to me, and come like a shaking storm on me, when I am about to conclude, from the marks of grace, which I seem to find in myself, that I am in the state of grace." *Answer.* These things should indeed stir us up to a most serious and impartial examination of ourselves; but ought not to keep us in a continued suspense as to our state. Sirs, you see the outside of hypocrites, their duties, their gifts, their tears, and so on, but you see not their inside; you do not discern their hearts, the bias of their spirits. Upon what you see of them, you found a judgment of charity as to their state; and you do well to judge charitably in such a case, because you cannot know the secret springs of their actions: but you are seeking, and ought to have, a judgment of certainty as to your own state; and therefore are to look into that part of religion; which none in the world but yourselves can discern in you; and which you can as little see in others. A hypocrite's region may appear far greater than that of a sincere soul: but that which makes the greatest figure in the eyes of men, is often of least worth before God. I would rather utter one of those groans which the apostle speaks of, Rom. viii. 26, than shed Esau's tears, have Balaam's prophetic spirit, or the joy of the stony-ground hearer. "The fire that shall try every man's work," will try, not of what bulk it is, but "of what sort it is," 1 Cor. iii. 13.—Though you may know what bulk of religion another has, and that it be more bulky than your own, yet God doth not regard that; why then do you make such a matter of it? It is impossible for you, without divine revelation, certainly to know of what sort another man's religion is: but you may certainly know what sort your own is of, without extraordinary revelation; otherwise the apostle would not exhort the saints to "give diligence to make their calling and election sure," 2 Peter i. 10. Therefore the attainments of hypocrites and apostates should not dsturb you, in your serious inquiry into your own state. I will tell you two things, wherein the meanest saints go beyond the most refined hypocrites: 1. In denying themselves; renouncing all confidence in themselves, and their own works; acquiescing in, being well pleased with, and venturing their souls upon, God's plan of salvation through Jesus Christ, Matt. v. 3, "Blessed are the poor in spirit, for theirs is the kingdom of heaven." And chap. xi. 6, "Blessed is he, whosoever shall not be offended in me." Phil. iii. 3, "We are the circumcision, which worship God in the spirit, and rejoice in Jesus Christ, and have no confidence in the flesh." 2. In a real hatred of all sin; being willing to part with every lust, without exception, and to comply with every duty which the Lord makes, or shall make known to them, Psalm cxix. 6, "Then shall I not be ashamed, when I have respect unto all thy commandments." Try yourselves by these.

Case 6. "I see myself fall so far short of the saints mentioned in the Scriptures, and of several excellent persons of my own acquaintance, that, when I look on them, I can hardly look on myself as one of the same family with them." *Answer.* It is indeed matter of humiliation, that we do not get forward to that measure of grace and holiness which we see is attainable in this life. This should make us more vigorously press towards the mark: but surely it is from the devil, that weak Christians make a rack for themselves, of the attainments of the strong. To yield to the temptation, is as unreasonable as for a child to dispute away his relation to his father, because he is not of the same stature with his elder brethren. There are saints of several sizes in Christ's family; some fathers, some young men, and some little children, 1 John ii. 13, 14.

Case 7. "I never read in the word of God, nor did I ever know of a child of God, so tempted, and so left of God, as I am; and therefore, no saint's case being like mine, I cannot but conclude that I am none of their number. *Answer.* This objection arises to some from their ignorance of the Scriptures, and the experience of Christians. It is profitable, in this case, to impart the matter to some experienced Christian friend, or to some godly minister. This has been a blessed means of peace to some persons; while their case, which appeared to them to be singular, has been proved to have been the case of other saints. The Scriptures give instances of very horrid temptations, wherewith the saints have been assaulted. Job was tempted to blaspheme; this was the great thing the devil aimed at in the case of that great saint, Job. i. 11, "He will curse thee to thy face." Chap. ii. 9, "Curse God and die." Asaph was tempted to think it was in vain to be religious, which was in effect to throw off all religion, Psalm lxxiii. 13, "Verily I have cleansed my heart in vain." Yea, Christ himself was tempted to "cast himself down from a pinnacle of the temple," and to "worship the devil," Matt. iv. 6—9. And many of the children of God have not only been attacked with, but have actually yielded to very gross temptation for a time. Peter denied Christ, and cursed and swore that he knew him not, Mark xiv. 71. Paul, when a persecutor compelled even saints to blaspheme, Acts xxvi. 10, 11. Many of the saints can, from their sad experience, bear witness to very gross temptations, which have astonished their spirits, made their very flesh to tremble, and sickened their bodies. Satan's fiery darts make terrible work; and will cost some pains to quench them, by a vigorous managing of the shield of faith, Eph. vi. 16. Sometimes he makes such desparate attacks, that never was one more put to it, in running to and fro, without intermission, to quench the fire-balls incessantly thrown into his house by an enemy, designing to burn the house about him, than the poor tempted saint is, to repel Satanical injections. But these injections, these horrid temptations though they are a dreadful affliction, they are not the sins of the tempted, unless they make them heirs by consenting to them. They will be charged upon the tempter alone, if they be not consented to; and will no more be laid to the charge of the tempted party, than a bastard's being laid down at a chaste man's door will fix guilt upon him.

But suppose neither minister nor private Christian, to whom you go, can tell you of any who has been in your case; yet you ought not thence to infer that your case is singular, far less to give up hope: for it is not to be thought, that every godly minister, or private Christian, has had experience of all the cases which a child of God may be in. We need not doubt that some have had distresses known only to God and their own consciences; and so to others these distresses are as if they had never been. Yea, and though the Scriptures contain suitable directions for every case which a child of God can be in, and these illustrated with a sufficient number of examples; yet it is not to be imagined that there are in the

Scriptures perfect instances of every particular case incident to the saints. Therefore, though you cannot find an instance of your case in the Scripture, yet bring your case to it, and you shall find suitable remedies prescribed there for it. Study rather to make use of Christ for your case, who has a remedy for all diseases, than to know if ever any was in your case. Though one should shew you an instance of your case, in an undoubted saint; yet none could promise that it would certainly give you ease: for a scrupulous conscience would readily find out some difference. And if nothing but a perfect conformity of another's case to yours will satisfy it will be hard, if not impossible, to satisfy you; for it is with people's cases, as with their natural faces: though the faces of all men are of one make, and some are so very like others, that, at first view, we are ready to take them for the same; yet if you view them more accurately, you will see something in every face, distinguishing it from all others; though possibly you cannot tell what it is. Wherefore I conclude, that if you can find in yourselves the marks of regeneration, proposed to you from the word, you ought to conclude you are in the state of grace, though your case were singular, which is indeed unlikely.

Case 8. "The afflictions I meet with are strange and unusual. I doubt if ever a child of God was tried with such dispensations of providence as I am." *Answer.* Much of what was said on the preceding case, may be helpful in this. Holy Job was assaulted with this temptation, Job v. 1, "To which of the saints wilt thou turn?" But he rejected it, and held fast his integrity. The apostle supposes that Christians may be tempted to "think it strange concerning the fiery trial," 1 Pet. iv. 12. But they have need of larger experience than Solomon's, who will venture to say, "See this is new," Eccl. i. 10. What though, in respect of the outward dispensations of providence, "it happen to you according to the work of the wicked?" yet you may be just notwithstanding; according to Solomon's observation, Eccl. viii. 14. Sometimes we travel in ways where we can neither perceive the prints of the foot of man or beast; yet we cannot from thence conclude that there was never any there before us: so though thou canst not perceive the footsteps of the flock, in the way of thine affliction, thou must not therefore conclude that thou art the first that ever travelled that road. But what if it were so? Some one saint or other must be first, in drinking of each bitter cup the rest have drunk of. What warrant have you or I to limit the Holy One of Israel to a trodden path, in his dispensations towards us? "Thy way is in the sea, and thy path in the great waters; and thy footsteps are not known," Psalm lxxvii. 19. If the Lord should carry you to heaven by some retired road, so to speak, you would have no ground of complaint. Learn to allow sovereignty a latitude; be at your duty; and let no affliction cast a veil over any evidences you otherwise have for your being in the state of grace: for "no man knoweth either love or hatred by all that is before him," Eccl. ix. 1.

Use II. You that are strangers to this new birth, be convinced of the absolute necessity of it. Are all who are in the state of grace born again? then you have neither part nor lot in it, who are not born again. I must tell you in the words of our Lord and Saviour, and O that he would speak them to your hearts! "You *must* be born again," John iii. 7. For your conviction, consider these few things.

1. Regeneration is absolutely necessary to qualify you to do any thing really good and acceptable to God. While you are not born again, your best works are but glittering sins; for though the matter of them is good, they are quite marred in the performance. Consider, 1. That without regeneration there is no faith, and "without faith it is impossible to please God," Heb. xi. 6. Faith is a vital act of the new-born soul. The evangelist, shewing the different entertainment which our Lord Jesus had from different persons, some receiving him, some rejecting him, points at regenerating grace as the true cause of that difference, without which never any one would have received him. He tells us, that "as many as received him," were those "which were born—of God," John i. 11— 13. Unregenerate men may presume; but true faith they cannot have. Faith is a flower that grows not in the field of nature. As the tree cannot grow without a root, neither can a man believe without the new nature, whereof the principle of believing is a part. 2. Without regeneration a man's works are dead works. As is the principle, so must the effects be: if the lungs are rotten, the breath will be unsavoury; and he who at best is dead in sin, his works at best will be but dead works. "Unto them that are defiled and unbelieving, is nothing pure—being abominable, and disobedient, and unto every good work reprobate," Tit. i. 15, 16. Could we say of a man, that he is more blameless in his life than any other in the world; that he reduces his body with fasting; and has made his knees as horns with continual praying; but he is not born again: that exception would mar all. As if one should say, There is a well proportioned body, but the soul is gone; it is but a dead lump. This is a melting consideration. Thou dost many things materially good; but God says, All these things avail not, as long as I see the old nature reigning in the man. Gal. vi. 15, "For in Jesus Christ

neither circumcision availeth any thing, nor uncircumcision, but a new creature."

If thou art not born again, (1.) All thy reformation is naught in the sight of God. Thou hast shut the door, but the thief is still in the house. It may be thou art not what once thou wast; yet thou art not what thou must be, if ever thou see heaven; for "except a man be born again, he cannot see the kingdom of God," John iii. 3. (2.) Thy prayers are an "abomination to the Lord," Prov. xv. 8. It may be, others admire thy seriousness; thou criest as for thy life; but God accounts of the opening of thy mouth, as one would account of the opening of a grave full of rottenness, Rom. iii. 13, "Their throat is an open sepulchre." Others are affected with thy prayers; which seem to them, as if they would rend the heavens; but God accounts them but as the howling of a dog: "They have not cried unto me with their hearts, when they howled upon their beds," Hos. vii. 14. Others take thee for a wrestler and prevailer with God; but he can take no delight in thee nor thy prayers, Isa. lxvi. 3, "He that killeth an ox, is as if he slew a man: he that sacrificeth a lamb, as if he cut off a dog's neck;—he that burneth incense, as if he blessed an idol." Why, because thou art yet "in the gall of bitterness, and bond of iniquity!" (3.) All thou hast done for God, and his cause in the world, though it may be followed with temporal rewards, yet it is lost as to divine acceptance. This is clear from the case of Jehu, who was indeed rewarded with a kingdom, for his executing due vengeance upon the house of Ahab; as being a work good for the matter of it, because it was commanded of God, as you may see, 2 Kings ix. 7; yet was he punished for it in his posterity, because he did it not in a right manner, Hos. i. 4, "I will avenge the blood of Jezreel upon the house of Jehu." God looks chiefly to the heart: and if so, truly, though the outward appearance be fairer than that of many others, yet the hidden man of thy heart is loathsome; you look well before men, but are not, as Moses was, fair to God, as the margin has it, Acts vii. 20. O what a difference is there between the characters of Asa and Amaziah! "The high places were not removed; nevertheless, Asa's heart was perfect with the Lord all his days," 1 Kings xv. 14. "Amaziah did that which was right in the sight of the Lord, but not with a perfect heart," 2 Chron. xxv. 2. It may be thou art zealous against sin in others, and dost admonish them of their duty, and reprove them for their sin; and they hate thee, because thou dost thy duty; but I must tell thee, God hates thee too, because thou dost it not in a right manner; and that thou canst never do, whilst thou art not born again. (4.) All thy struggles against sin in thine own heart and life, are naught. The proud Pharisee afflicted his body with fasting, and God struck his soul, in the mean time, with a sentence of condemnation, Luke xviii. Balaam struggled with his covetous temper, to that degree, that though he loved the wages of unrighteousness, yet he would not win them by cursing Israel: but he died the death of the wicked, Numb. xxxi. 8. All thou dost, while in an unregenerate state, is for thyself: therefore it will fare with thee as with a subject, who having reduced the rebels, puts the crown on his own head, and loses all his good service and his head too.

Objection. "If it be thus with us, then we need never perform any religious duty at all." *Answer.* The conclusion is not just. No inability of thine can excuse from the duty which God's law lays on thee: and there is less evil in doing thy duty, than there is in the omission of it. But there is a difference between omitting a duty, and doing it as thou dost it. A man orders the masons to build him a house. If they quite neglect the work, that will not be accepted; if they build on the old rotten foundation, neither will that please: but they must raze the foundation, and build on firm ground. "Go thou and do likewise." In the mean time, it is not in vain even for thee to seek the Lord: for though he regards thee not, yet he may have respect to his own ordinances, and do thee good thereby, as was said before.

2. Without regeneration there is no communion with God. There is a society on earth, whose "fellowship is with the Father, and with his Son Jesus Christ," 1 John i. 3. But out of that society, all the unregenerate are excluded; for they are all enemies to God, as you heard before at large. Now, "can two walk together, except they be agreed?" Amos iii. 3. They are all unholy: and "what communion hath light with darkness—Christ with Belial?" 2 Cor. vi. 14, 15. They may have a shew and semblance of holiness; but they are strangers to true holiness, and therefore "without God in the world." How sad is it, to be employed in religious duties, yet to have no fellowship with God in them! You would not be content with your meat, unless it nourished you; nor with your clothes, unless they kept you warm: and how can you satisfy yourselves with your duties, while you have no communion with God in them?

3. Regeneration is absolutely necessary to qualify you for heaven. None go to heaven but those who are made meet for it, Col. i. 12. As it was with Solomon's temple, 1 Kings vi. 7, so is it with the temple above. It is "built of stone made ready before it is brought thither;" namely, of "lively stones," 1 Pet. ii. 5,— "wrought for the selfsame thing," 2 Cor. v. 5; for they cannot be

laid in that glorious building just as they come out of the quarry of depraved nature. Jewels of gold are not meet for swine, and far less jewels of glory for unrenewed sinners. Beggars, in their rags, are not fit for kings' houses; nor sinners to enter into the King's palace, without the raiment of needlework, Psalm xlv. 14, 15. What wise man would bring fish out of the water to feed in his meadows? or send his oxen to feed in the sea? Even as little are the unregenerate fit for heaven, or heaven fit for them. It would never be relished by them.

The unregenerate would find fault with heaven on several accounts. As, (1.) That it is a strange country. Heaven is the renewed man's native country: his Father is in heaven; his mother is Jerusalem, which is above, Gal. iv. 26. He is born from above, John iii. 3. Heaven is his home, 2 Cor. v. 1 ; therefore he looks on himself as a stranger on this earth, and his heart is homeward, Heb. xi. 16, "They desire a better country, that is, a heavenly country." But the unregenerate man is the man of the earth, Psalm x. 18; written in the earth, Jer. xvii. 13. Now, "Home is home, be it ever so homely:" therefore he minds earthly things, Phil. iii. 19. There is a peculiar sweetness in our native soil; and with difficulty are men drawn to leave it, and dwell in a strange country. In no case does that prevail more than in this; for unrenewed men would quit their pretensions to heaven, were it not that they see they cannot make a better bargain. (2.) There is nothing in heaven that they delight in, as agreeable to the carnal heart, Rev. xxi. 27, "For there shall in no wise enter into it any thing that defileth." When Mahomet gave out a paradise to be a place of sensual delights, his religion was greedily embraced; for that is the heaven men naturally choose. If the covetous man could get bags full of gold there, and the voluptuous man could promise himself his sensual delights they might be reconciled to heaven, and meetened for it too; but since it is not so, though they may utter fair words about it, truly it has little of their hearts. (3.) Every corner there is filled with that which of all things they have the least liking for; and that is holiness, true holiness, perfect holiness. Were one that abhors swine's flesh, bidden to a feast where all the dishes were of that sort of meat, but variously prepared, he would find fault with every dish at the table, notwithstanding all the art used to make them palatable. It is true, there is joy in heaven, but it is holy joy; there are pleasures in heaven, but they are holy pleasures; there are places in heaven, but it is holy ground,—that holiness which in every place, and in every thing there, would mar all to the unregenerate. (4.) Were they carried thither, they would not only change their place, which would be a great heart-break, but they would change their company too. Truly, they would never like the company there, who care not for communion with God here; nor value the fellowship of his people, at least in the vitals of practical godliness. Many, indeed, mix themselves with the godly on earth, to procure a name to themselves, and to cover the sinfulness of their hearts; but that trade cannot be managed there. (5.) They would never like the employment of heaven, they care so little for it now. The business of the saints there would be an intolerable burden to them, seeing it is not agreeable to their nature. To be taken up in beholding, admiring, and praising him that sits on the throne, and the Lamb, would be work unsuitable, and therefore unsavoury to an unrenewed soul. (6.) They would find this fault with it, that the whole is of everlasting continuance. This would be a killing ingredient in it to them. How would such as now account the Sabbath day a burden, brook the celebration of an everlasting Sabbath in the heavens!

4. Regeneration is absolutely necessary to your being admitted into heaven, John iii. 3. No heaven without it. Though carnal men could digest all those things which make heaven so unsuitable for them, yet God will never bring them thither. Therefore born again you must be, else you shall never see heaven; you shall perish eternally. For, (1.) There is a bill of exclusion against you in the court of heaven, and against all of your sort; "Except a man be born again, he cannot see the kingdom of God," John iii. 3. Here is a bar before you, that men and angels cannot remove. To hope for heaven, in the face of this peremptory sentence, is to hope that God will recall his word, and sacrifice his truth and faithfulness to your safety; which is infinitely more than to hope that "the earth shall be forsaken for you, and the rock removed out of its place." (2.) There is no holiness without regeneration. It is "the new man which is created in true holiness," Eph. iv. 24. And no heaven without holiness; for "without holiness no man shall see the Lord," Heb. xii. 14. Will the gates of pearl be opened, to let in dogs and and swine? No; their place is without, Rev. xxii. 15. God will not admit such into the holy place of communion with him here; and will he admit them into the holiest of all hereafter? Will he take the children of the devil, and permit them to sit with him in his throne? Or, will he bring the unclean into the city, whose street is pure gold? Be not deceived; grace and glory are but two links of one chain, which God has joined, and no man shall put asunder. None are transplanted into the paradise above, but out of the nursery of grace below. If you be unholy while in this world, you

will be for ever miserable in the world to come. (3.) All the unregenerate are without Christ, and therefore have no hope while in that case, Eph. ii. 12. Will Christ prepare mansions of glory for those who refuse to receive him into their hearts? Nay, rather will he not "laugh at their calamity," who now "set at nought all his counsel?" Prov. i. 25, 26. (4.) There is an infallible connexion between a finally unregenerate state and damnation, arising from the nature of the things themselves; and from the decree of heaven which is fixed and immovable, as mountains of brass, John iii. 3; Rom. viii. 6. "To be carnally minded is death." An unregenerate state is hell in the bud. It is eternal destruction in embryo, growing daily, though thou dost not discern it. Death is painted on many a fair face, in this life. Depraved nature makes men meet to be partakers of the inheritance of the damned, in utter darkness. 1. The heart of stone within thee, is a sinking weight. As a stone naturally goes downward, so the hard stony heart tends downward to the bottomless pit. You are hardened against reproof; though you are told your danger, yet you will not see it, you will not believe it. But remember that the conscience being now seared with a hot iron, is a sad presage of everlasting burnings. 2. Your unfruitfulness under the means of grace, fits you for the axe of God's judgments, Matt. iii. 10, "Every tree that bringeth not forth good fruit, is hewn down, and cast into the fire." The withered branch is fuel for the fire, John xv. 6. Tremble at this, you despisers of the Gospel: if you be not thereby made meet for heaven, you will be like the barren ground, bearing briers and thorns, "nigh unto cursing, whose end is to be burned," Heb. vi. 8. 3. The hellish dispositions of mind, which discover themselves in profanity of life, fit the guilty for the regions of horror. A profane life will have a miserable end. "They which do such things, shall not inherit the kingdom of God," Gal. v. 19—21. Think on this, you prayerless persons, ye mockers of religion, ye cursers and swearers, ye unclean and unjust persons, who have not so much as moral honesty to keep you from lying, cheating, and stealing. What sort of a tree do you think it is, upon which these fruits grow? Is it a tree of righteousness, which the Lord hath planted? Or is it not such a one as cumbers the ground, which God will pluck up for fuel to the fire of his wrath? 4. Your being dead in sin, makes you meet to be wrapped in flames of brimstone, as a winding-sheet; and to be buried in the bottomless pit, as in a grave. Great was the cry in Egypt, when the first-born in each family was dead; but are there not many families, where all are dead together? Nay, many there are who are twice dead, plucked up by the root. Sometimes in their life they have been roused by apprehensions of death, and its consequences; but now they are so far on in their way to the land of darkness, that they hardly ever have the least glimmering of light from heaven. 5. The darkness of your minds presages eternal darkness. O the horrid ignorance with which some are plagued; while others, who have got some rays of the light of reason in their heads, are utterly void of spiritual light in their hearts! If you knew your case, you would cry out, Oh! darkness! darkness! darkness! makmaking way for the blackness of darkness for ever! The face-covering is upon you already, as condemned persons; so near are you to everlasting darkness. It is only Jesus Christ who can stop the execution, pull the napkin off the face of the condemned malefactor, and put a pardon in his hand, Isa. xxv. 7. "He will destroy, in this mountain, the face of covering cast over all people," that is, the face-covering cast over the condemned, as in Haman's case, Esth. vii. 8. "As the word went out of the king's mouth, they covered Haman's face." 6. The chains of darkness you are bound with in the prison of your depraved state, Isa. lxi. 1, fits you to be cast into the burning fiery furnace. Ah, miserable men! Sometimes their consciences stir within them, and they begin to think of amending their ways. But alas! they are in chains, they cannot do it. They are chained by the heart: their lusts cleave so fast to them, that they cannot, nay, they will not shake them off. Thus you see what affinity there is between an unregenerate state, and the state of the damned, the state of absolute and irretrievable misery. Be convinced, then, that you must be born again; put a high value on the new birth, and eagerly desire it.

The text tells you, that the word is the seed, whereof the new creature is formed: therefore take heed to it, and entertain it, as it is your life. Apply yourself to the reading of the Scriptures. You that cannot read, get others to read it to you. Wait diligently on the preaching of the word, as by divine appointment the special mean of conversion; "for—it pleased God, by the foolishness of preaching, to save them that believe," 1 Cor. i. 21. Wherefore cast not yourselves out of Christ's way; reject not the means of grace, lest you be found to judge yourselves unworthy of eternal life. Attend carefully to the word preached. Hear every sermon, as if you were hearing for eternity; take heed that the fowls of the air pick not up this seed from you, as it is sown. "Give thyself wholly to it," 1 Tim. iv. 15. "Receive it not as the word of men, but, as it is in truth, the word of God," 1 Thess. ii. 13. Hear it with application, looking on it as a message sent from heaven, to you in particular; though not to you only, Rev. iii. 22. "He that hath an ear, let him hear what the Spirit saith unto the churches." Lay it up in your hearts; meditate upon it; and be not as the unclean beasts, that chew not the cud. But by earnest prayer, beg that the dew of Heaven may fall on thy heart, that the seed may spring up there.

More particularly, 1 Receive the testimony of the word of God, concerning the misery of an unregenerate state, the sinfulness thereof, and the absolute necessity of regeneration. 2. Receive its testimony concerning God, what a holy and just One he is. 3. Examine thy ways by it; namely, the thoughts of thy heart, the expressions of thy lips, and the tenour of thy life. Look back through the several periods of thy life; and see thy sins from the precepts of the word, and learn, from its threatening, what thou art liable to on account of these sins. 4. By the help of the same word of God, view the corruption of thy nature, as in a glass which manifests our ugly face in a clear manner. Were these things deeply rooted in the heart, they might be the seed of that fear and sorrow, on account of thy soul's state, which are necessary to prepare and stir thee up to look after a Saviour. Fix your thoughts upon him offered to thee in the Gospel, as fully suited to thy case; having, by his obedience unto death, perfectly satisfied the justice of God, and brought in everlasting righteousness. This may prove the seed of humiliation, desire, hope and faith; and move thee to stretch out the withered hand unto him, at his own command.

Let these things sink deeply into your hearts, and improve them diligently. Remember, whatever you are, you *must* be born again; else it had been better for you, that you had never been born. Wherefore, if any of you shall live and die in an unregenerate state, you will be inexcusable, having been fairly warned of your danger.

PART II.

MYSTICAL UNION BETWEEN CHRIST AND BELIEVERS.

I am the vine ye are the branches.—JOHN XV. 5.

Having spoken of the change made by regeneration, on all those who will inherit eternal life, in opposition to their natural real state, the state of degeneracy; I proceed to speak of the change made on them, in their union with the Lord Jesus Christ, in opposition to their natural relative state, the state of misery. The doctrine of the saints' union with Christ, is very plainly and fully insisted on, from the beginning to the eighth verse of this chapter; which is a part of our Lord's farewell sermon to his disciples. Sorrow had now filled their hearts; they were apt to say, Alas! what will become of us, when our Master is taken from our head? Who will then instruct us? Who will solve our doubts? How shall we be supported under our difficulties and discouragements? How shall we be able to live without our wonted communication with him? Therefore our Lord Jesus Christ seasonably teaches them the mystery of their union with him, comparing himself to the vine, and them to the branches.

He compares, 1. Himself to a vine. "I am the vine." He had been celebrating, with his disciples, the sacrament of his supper, that sign and seal of his people's union with him; and had told them, "That he would drink no more of the fruit of the vine, till he should drink it new with them in his Father's kingdom:" and now he shews himself to be the vine, from whence the wine of their consolation should come. The vine has less beauty than many other trees, but it is exceedingly fruitful; fitly representing the low condition in which our Lord was in, bringing many sons to glory. But that which is chiefly aimed at, in his comparing himself to a vine, is to represent himself as the supporter and nourisher of his people, in whom they live and bring forth fruit. 2. He compares them to branches; ye are the branches of that vine. Ye are the branches knit to, and growing on this stock, drawing all your life and sap from it. It is a beautiful comparison; as if he had said, I am as a vine, you are as the branches of that vine. Now there are two sorts of branches: 1. Natural branches, which at first spring out of the stock. These are the branches that are in the tree, and were never out of it. 2. There are ingrafted branches, which are branches cut off from the tree that first gave them life, and put into another, to grow upon it. Thus branches come to be on a tree, which originally were not on it. The branches mentioned in the text, are of the latter sort; branches broken off, as the word in the original language denotes, namely, from the tree that first gave them life. None of the children of men are natural branches of the second Adam, that is, Jesus Christ, the true vine; they are the natural branches of the first Adam, that degenerate vine: but the elect are all of them, sooner or later, broken off from their natural stock, and ingrafted into Christ, the true vine.

DOCTRINE. They who are in the state of grace, are ingrafted in, and united to, the Lord Jesus Christ. They are taken out of their natural stock, cut off from it; and are now ingrafted into Christ, as the new stock.

In general, for understanding the union between the Lord Jesus Christ and his elect, who believe in him, and on him, I observe,

1. It is a spiritual union. Man and wife, by their marriage-union, become one flesh; Christ and true believers, by this union, become one spirit, 1 Cor. vi. 17. As one soul or spirit actuates both the head and the members in the natural body, so the one Spirit of God dwells in Christ and the Christian; for, "if any man have not the Spirit of Christ, he is none of his his," Rom. viii. 9. Earthly union is made by contact; so the stones in a building are united; but this is a union of another nature. Were it possible that we could eat the flesh and drink the blood of Christ, in a corporeal and carnal manner, it would profit nothing, John vi. 63. It was not Mary's bearing him in her womb, but her believing on him, that made her a saint, Luke xi. 27, 28, "A certain woman—said unto him, Blessed is the womb that bare thee, and the paps which thou hast sucked. But he said, Yea, rather, blessed are they that hear the word of God, and keep it."

2. It is a real union. Such is our weakness in our present state, so much are we sunk in sin, that in our fancy, we are prone to form an image of every thing proposed to us: and as to whatever is denied us, we are apt to suspect it to be only a fiction. But nothing is more real than what is spiritual: as approaching nearest to the nature of him who is the fountain of all reality, namely, God himself. We do not see with our eyes the union between our own soul and body; neither can we represent it to ourselves truly, by imagination, as we do sensible things: yet the reality of it is not to be doubted. Faith is no fancy, but "the substance of things hoped for," Heb. xi. 1. Neither is the union thereby made between Christ and believers imaginary, but most real: "For we are members of his body, of his flesh, and of his bones," Eph. v. 30.

2. It is a most close and intimate union. Believers, regenerate persons, who believe in him, and rely on him, have put on Christ, Gal. iii. 27. If that be not enough, he is in them, John xvii. 23, formed in them as the child in the womb, Gal. iv. 19. He is the foundation, 1 Cor. iii. 11; they are the lively stones built upon him, 1 Pet. ii. 5. He is the head and they the body, Eph. i. 22, 23. Nay, he liveth in them, as their very souls live in their bodies, Gal. ii. 20. And what is more than all this, they are one in the Father and the Son, as the Father is in Christ, and Christ in the Father, John xvii. 21, "That they all may be one; as thou Father art in me, and I in thee, that they also may be one in us."

4. Though it is not a mere legal union, yet it is a union supported by law. Christ, as the surety, and Christians as the princi-

pal debtors, are one in the eye of the law. When the elect had run themselves, with the rest of mankind, in debt to the justice of God, Christ became surety for them, and paid the debt. When they believe on him, they are united to him in a spiritual marriage union; which takes effect so far, that what he did and suffered for them is reckoned in law, as if they had done and suffered it themselves. Hence, they are said to be crucified with Christ, Gal. ii. 20; buried with him, Col. ii. 12; yea, raised up together, namely, with Christ, " and made to sit together in heavenly places in Christ Jesus," Eph. ii. 6. In which places, saints on earth, of whom the apostle there speaks, cannot be said to be sitting, but in the way of law reckoning.

5. It is an indissolute union. Once in Christ, ever in him. Having taken up his habitation in the heart, he never removes. None can untie this happy knot.—Who will dissolve this union? Will he himself? No, he will not; we have his word for it; "I will not turn away from them," Jer. xxxii. 40. But perhaps the sinner will do this mischief to himself? No, he shall not; "they shall not depart from me," saith their God. Can devils do it? No, unless they be stronger than Christ and his Father too; "Neither shall any man pluck them out of my hand," saith our Lord, John x. 28. " And none is able to pluck them out of my Father's hand," verse 30. But what say you of death, which parts husband and wife; yea, separates the soul from the body? Will not death do it? No: the apostle, Rom. viii. 38, 39, is " persuaded that neither death," terrible as it is, " nor life," desirable as it is ; " nor" devils, those evil " angels, nor" the devil's persecuting agents, though they be " principalities, nor powers" on earth ; " nor" evil " things present," already lying on us; " nor" evil " things to come" on us ; " nor" the " height" of worldly felicity; " nor depth" of worldly misery ; " nor any other creature," good or evil, " shall be able to separate us from the love of God, which is Christ Jesus our Lord." As death separated Christ's soul from his body, but could not separate either his soul or body from his divine nature; so, though the saints should be separated from their nearest relations in the world, and from all their earthly enjoyments; yea, though their souls should be separated from their bodies separated in a thousand pieces, their " bones scattered, as one cutteth or cleaveth wood ;" yet soul and body shall remain united to the Lord Christ; for even in death, "they sleep in Jesus," 1 Thess. iv. 14; and " he keepeth all their bones," Psalm xxxiv. 20. Union with Christ, is " the grace wherein we stand," firm and stable, " as Mount Zion, which cannot be removed."

6. It is a mysterious union. The gospel is a doctrine of mysteries. It discovers to us the substantial union of the three persons in one Godhead, 1 John v. 7, "These three are one;" the hypostatical union, of the divine and human natures, in the person of the Lord Jesus Christ, 1 Tim. iii. 16, "God was manifest in the flesh;" and the mystical union, between Christ and believers; "This is a great mystery" also, Eph. v. 32. O what mysteries are here! The head in heaven, the members on earth, yet really united! "Christ in the believer, living in him, walking in him:" and "the believer dwelling in God, putting on the Lord Jesus, eating his flesh, and drinking his blood!" This makes the saints a mystery to the world; yea, a mystery to themselves.

I come now more particularly to speak of this union with, and ingrafting into, Jesus Christ.

I. I shall consider the natural stock, which the branches are taken out of.

II. The supernatural stock they are ingrafted into.

III. What branches are cut off the old stock, and put into the new.

IV. How it is done. And,

V. The benefits flowing from this union and ingrafting.

I. Let us take a view of the stock, which the branches are taken out of. The two Adams, that is, Adam and Christ, are the two stocks: for the Scripture speaks of these two, as if there had been no more men in the world than they, 1 Cor. xv. 45, "The first man Adam was made a living soul, the last Adam was made a quickening spirit;" verse 47, "The first man is of the earth earthy: the second man is the Lord from heaven." And the reason is, there never were any that were not branches of one of these two; all men being either in the one stock or in the other: for in these two sorts all mankind stand divided, verse 48, "As is the earthy, such are they also which are earthy; and as is the heavenly, such are they also that are heavenly." The first Adam then, is the natural stock: on this stock are the branches found growing at first, which are afterwards cut off, and ingrafted into Christ. As for the fallen angels, as they had no relation to the first Adam, so they have none to the second.

There are four things to be remembered here. (1.) That all mankind, the man Christ excepted, are naturally branches of the first Adam, Rom. v. 12, "By one man sin entered into the world, and death by sin: and so death passed upon all men." (2.) The bond which knit us unto the natural stock, was the covenant of works. Adam, being our natural root, was made the moral root also, bearing all his posterity, as representing them in the covenant of works. For " by one man's disobedience many were made sinners," Rom. v. 19. It was necessary that there should be a peculiar relation between that one man and the many, as a foundation for imputing his sin to them. This relation did not arise from the mere natural bond between him and us, as a father to his children; for so we are related to our immediate parents, whose sins are not thereupon imputed to us, as Adam's sin is, but it arose from a moral bond between Adam and us: the bond of a covenant, which could be no other than the covenant of works, wherein we are united to him, as branches to a stock. Hence Jesus Christ, though a son of Adam, Luke iii. 23—38, was none of these branches; for as he came not of Adam, in virtue of the blessing of marriage, which was given before the fall, Gen. i. 28, " Be fruitful, and multiply," &c. but in virtue of a special promise made after the fall, Gen. iii. 15, " The seed of the woman shall bruise the serpent's head," he could not be represented by Adam in a covenant made before his fall. (3.) As it is impossible for a branch to be in two stocks at once, so no man can be at one and the same time, both in the first and second Adam. (4.) Hence it evidently follows, that all who are not ingrafted in Jesus Christ, are yet branches of the old stock; and so partake of the nature of the same. Now, as to the first Adam, our natural stock, consider,

First, What a stock he was originally. He was a vine of the Lord's planting, a choice vine, a noble vine, wholly good. There was a consultation of the Trinity at the planting of this vine, Gen. i. 26, " Let us make man in our image, after our own likeness." There was no rottenness at the heart of it. There was sap and juice enough in it to have nourished all the branches, to bring forth fruit unto God. My meaning is, Adam was made able perfectly to keep the commandments of God, which would have procured eternal life to himself, and to all his posterity; for as all die by Adam's disobedience, all would have had life by his obedience, if he had stood. Consider,

Secondly, What that stock now is. Ah! most unlike to what it was when planted by the Author of all good. A blast from hell, and a bite with the venomous teeth of the old serpent, have made it a degenerate stock; a dead stock; nay, a killing stock.

1. It is a degenerate evil stock. Therefore the Lord God said to Adam in that dismal day, " Where art thou?" Gen. iii. 9. In what condition art thou now? " How art thou turned into the degenerate plant of a strange vine unto me!" Or, " Where wast thou?" Why not in the place of meeting with me? Why so long

in coming? What means this fearful change; this hiding of thyself from me? Alas! the stock is degenerate, quite spoiled, is become altogether naught, and brings forth wild grapes. Converse with the devil is preferred to communion with God. Satan is believed; and God, who is truth itself, disbelieved. He who was the friend of God is now in conspiracy against him. Darkness is come in the place of light; ignorance prevails in the mind, where divine knowledge shone; the will, which was righteous and regular, is now turned rebel against its Lord: and the whole man is in dreadful disorder.

Before I go farther, let me stop and observe, Here is a mirror both for saints and sinners. Sinners, stand here and consider what you are; and saints, learn what you once were. You, sinners, are branches of a degenerate stock. Fruit you may bear indeed; but now that your vine is the vine of Sodom, your grapes must of course be grapes of gall, Deut. xxxii. 32. The Scripture speaks of two sorts of fruit which grow on the branches of the natural stock; and it is plain that they are of the nature of their degenerate stock. (1.) The wild grapes of wickedness, Isa. v. 2. These grow in abundance, by influence from hell. See Gal. v. 19—21. At its gates are all manner of these fruits, both new and old. Storms come from heaven to check them; but still they grow. They are struck at with the sword of the Spirit, the word of God; conscience gives them many a secret blow; yet they thrive. (2.) Fruit to themselves, Hos. x. 1. What else are all the unrenewed man's acts of obedience, his reformation, sober deportment, his prayers, and good works? They are all done chiefly for himself, not for the glory of God. These fruits are like the apples of Sodom, fair to look at, but full of ashes when handled and tried. You think you have not only the leaves of a profession, but the fruits of a holy practice too; but if you be not broken off from the old stock, and ingrafted in Christ Jesus, God accepts not, and regards not your fruits.

Here I must take occasion to tell you, there are five faults will be found in heaven with your best fruits.—1. Their bitterness; your "clusters are bitter," Deut. xxxii. 32. There is a spirit of bitterness, wherewith some come before the Lord, in religious duties, living in malice and envy; and which some professors entertain against others, because they outshine them in holiness of life, or because they are not of their opinion. This, wherever it reigns, is a fearful symptom of an unregenerate state. But I do not so much mean this, as that which is common to all the branches of the old stock, namely, the leaves of hypocrisy, Luke xii. 1, which sours and imbitters every duty they perform. Wisdom, that is full of good fruits, is without hypocrisy, James iii. 17. 2. Their ill savour. Their works are abominable, for they themselves are corrupt, Psalm xiv. 1. They all savour of the old stock, not of the new. It is the peculiar privilege of the saints, that they are unto God a sweet savour of Christ, 2 Cor. ii. 15. The unregenerate man's fruits savour not of love to Christ, nor of the blood of Christ, nor of the incense of his intercession, and therefore will never be accepted in heaven. 3. Their unripeness. Their grape is an unripe grape, Job xv. 33. There is no influence on them from the Sun of righteousness to bring them to perfection. They have the shape of fruit, but no more. The matter of duty is in them, but they want right principles and ends: their works are not in God, John iii. 21. Their prayers drop from their lips, before their hearts are impregnated with the vital sap of the Spirit of supplication: their tears fall from their eyes before their hearts are truly softened; their feet turn to new paths, and their way is altered, while their nature still is unchanged. 4. Their lightness. Being weighed in the balances, they are found wanting, Dan. v. 27. For evidence whereof you may observe that they do not humble the soul, but lift it up in pride. The good fruits of holiness bear down the branches they grow upon, making them to salute the ground, 1 Cor. xv. 19, "I laboured more abundantly than they all: yet not I, but the grace of God which was with me." But the blasted fruits of unrenewed men's performances, hang lightly on branches towering up to heaven, Judges xvii. 13, "Now know I, that the Lord will do me good, seeing I have a Levite to my priest." They look indeed too high for God to behold them: "Wherefore have we fasted, say they, and thou seest not?" Isa. lviii. 3. The more duties they do, and the better they seem to perform them, the less are they humbled, and the more are they lifted up. This disposition of the sinner is the exact reverse of what is to be found in the saint. To men, who neither are in Christ, nor are solicitous to be found in him, their duties are like floating bladders, wherewith they think to swim ashore to Immanuel's land; but these must needs break, and they consequently sink; because they take not Christ for the lifter up of their heads, Psalm iii. 3, 5. They are not all manner of pleasant fruits, Cant. vii. 13. Christ, as a king, must be served with variety. Where God makes the heart his garden, he plants it as Solomon did his, with trees of all kinds of fruits Eccl. ii. 5. Accordingly it brings forth the fruit of the Spirit in all goodness, Eph. v. 9. But the ungodly are not so; their obedience is never universal; there is always some one thing or other excepted. In one word, their fruits are fruits of an ill tree, that cannot be accepted in heaven.

2. Our natural stock is a dead stock, according to the threatening, Gen. ii. 17, "In the day thou eatest thereof, thou shalt surely die." Our root is now rottenness, no wonder the blossom goes up as dust. The stroke has gone to the heart, the sap is let out, and the tree is withered. The curse of the first covenant, like a hot thunderbolt from heaven, has lighted on it, and ruined it. It is cursed now as that fig-tree, Matth. xxi. 19, "Let no fruit grow on thee henceforward for ever." Now it is good for nothing, but to cumber the ground, and furnish fuel for Tophet.

Let me enlarge a little here also. Every unrenewed man is a branch of a dead stock. When thou seest, O sinner, a dead stock of a tree, exhausted of all its sap, having branches on it in the same condition, look on it as a lively representation of thy soul's state. 1. Where the stock is dead, the branches must needs be barren. Alas! the barrenness of many professors plainly discovers on what stock they are growing. It is easy to pretend to faith, but "shew me thy faith without thy works!" if thou canst, James ii. 18. 2. A dead stock can convey no sap to the branches, to make them bring forth fruit. The covenant of works was the bond of our union with the natural stock; but now it is become weak through the flesh; that is, through the degeneracy and depravity of human nature, Rom. viii. 3. It is strong enough to command, and to bind heavy burdens on the shoulders of those who are not in Christ, but it affords no strength to bear them. The sap, that was once in the root, is now gone: the law, like a merciless creditor, apprehends Adam's heirs, saying to each, "Pay what thou owest;" when, alas! his effects are riotously spent. 3. All pains and cost are lost on the tree, whose life is gone. In vain do men labour to get fruit on the branches, when there is no sap in the root. The gardener's pains are lost: ministers lose their labour on the branches of the old stock, while they continue on it. Many sermons are preached to no purpose; because there is no life to give sensation. Sleeping men may be awakened; but the dead cannot be raised without a miracle; even so the dead sinner must remain, if he be not restored to life by a miracle of grace. The influences of heaven are lost on such a tree: in vain doth the rain fall upon it; in vain is it laid open to the winter cold and frosts. The Lord of the vineyard digs about many a dead soul, but it is not bettered. "Bruise the fool in a mortar, his folly will not depart." Though he meets with many crosses, yet he retains his lusts: let him be laid on a sick bed, he will lie there like a sick beast, groaning under his pain, but not mourning for, nor turning from, his sin. Let death itself stare him in the face, he will presumptuously maintain his hope, as if he would look the grim messenger out of countenance. Sometimes there are common operations of the divine Spirit performed on him: he is sent home with a trembling heart, and with arrows of conviction sticking in his soul: but at length he prevails against these things, and becomes as secure as ever. Summer and winter are alike to the branches on the dead stock. When others about them are budding, blossoming, and bringing forth fruit, there is no change on them: the dead stock has no growing time at all. Perhaps it may be difficult to know, in the winter, what trees are dead, and what are alive; but the spring plainly discovers it. There are some seasons wherein there is little life to be perceived, even among saints; yet times of reviving come at length. But even when "the vine flourisheth, and the pomegranates bud forth," when saving grace is discovering itself by its lively actings wherever it is, the branches on the old stock are still withered. When the dry bones are coming together, bone to bone amongst saints, the sinner's bones are still lying about the grave's mouth. They are trees that cumber the ground, ready to be cut down; and will be cut down for the fire, if God in mercy prevent it not by cutting them off from that stock, and ingrafting them into another.

3. Our natural stock is a killing stock. If the stock die, how can the branches live? If the sap be gone from the root and heart, the branches must needs wither. "In Adam all die," 1 Cor. xv. 22. The root died in Paradise, and all the branches in it, and with it. The root is poisoned, and from thence the branches are infected; "death is in the pot;" and all that taste of the pulse, or pottage, are killed.

Know then, that every natural man is a branch of a killing stock. Our natural root not only gives us no life, but it has a killing power, reaching to all the branches thereof. There are four things which the first Adam conveys to all his branches, and they are abiding in, and lying on, such of them as are not ingrafted in Christ. 1. A corrupt nature. He sinned, and his nature was thereby corrupted and depraved; and this corruption is conveyed to all his posterity. He was infected, and the contagion spread itself over all his seed. 2. Guilt, that is, an obligation to punishment, Rom. v. 12, "By one man sin entered into the world, and death by sin; and so death passed upon all men, for that all have sinned." The threatenings of the law, as cords of death, are twisted about the branches of the old stock, to draw them over the hedge into the fire. And till they be cut off from this stock by the pruning-knife, the sword of vengeance hangs over their heads, to cut them down. 3. This killing stock transmits the curse into the branches. The stock, as the stock, (for I speak not of Adam in his personal and private capacity,) being cursed, so are the branches, Gal. iii. 10, " For as many as are of the works of the law, are under the curse." The curse affects the whole man, and all that belongs to him, every thing he possesses ; and worketh three ways. 1. As poison, infecting ; thus their blessings are cursed, Mal. ii. 2. Whatever the man enjoys, it can do him no good, but evil, being thus poisoned by the curse. His prosperity in the world destroys him, Prov. i. 32. The ministry of the gospel is a savour of death unto death to him, 2 Cor. ii. 16. His seeming attainments in religion are cursed to him ; his knowledge serves but to puff him up, and his duties to keep him back from Christ. 2. It worketh as a moth, consuming and wasting by little and little, Hos. v. 12, " Therefore will I be unto Ephraim as a moth." There is a worm at the root, consuming them by degrees. Thus the curse pursued Saul, till it wormed him out of all his enjoyments, and out of the very shew he had of religion. Sometimes they decay like the fat of lambs, and melt away as the show in the sunshine. 3. It acts as a lion rampant, Hos. v. 14, " I will be unto Ephraim as a lion." The Lord " rains on them snares, fire and brimstone, and an horrible tempest," in such a manner, that they are hurried away with the stream. He tears their enjoyments from them in his wrath, persues them with terrors, rends their souls from their bodies, and throws the dead branch into the fire. Thus the curse devours like fire, which none can quench. 4. This killing stock transmits death to the branches upon it. Adam took the poisonous cup, and drank it off: this occasioned death to himself and us. We came into the world spiritually dead, thereby exposed to eternal death, and absolutely liable to temporal death. This root is to us like the Scythian river, which, they say, brings forth little bladders every day, out of which come certain small flies, that are bred in the morning, winged at noon, and dead at night : a very lively emblem of our mortal state.

Now, sirs, is it not absolutely necessary to be broken off from this our natural stock ? What will our fair leaves of a profession, or our fruits of duties, avail, if we be still branches of the degenerate, dead, and killing stock ?—But, alas ! of the many questions among us, few are taken up about these, " Whether am I broken off from the old stock, or not ? Am I ingrafted in Christ, or not ?"—Ah ! wherefore all this waste of time ? Why is there so much noise about religion among many, who can give no good account of their having laid a good foundation, being mere strangers to experimental religion? I fear, if God does not in mercy undermine the religion of many of us, and let us see that we have none at all, our root will be found rottenness, and our blossom go up as dust, in a dying hour. Therefore let us look to our state, that we be not found fools in our latter end.

II. Let us now view the supernatural stock, into which the branches cut off from the natural stock are ingrafted. Jesus Christ is sometimes called "The Branch," Zech. iii. 8. So he is in respect of his human nature, being a branch, and the top branch, of the house of David. Sometimes he is called a Root, Isa. xi. 10. We have both together, Rev. xxi. 16, "I am the root and the offspring of David;" David's root as God, and his offspring as man. The text tells us, that he is the vine, that is, he, as a Mediator, is the vine stock, whereof believers are the branches. As the sap comes from the earth into the root and stock, and from thence is diffused into the branches; so, by Christ as Mediator, divine life is conveyed from the fountain, unto those who are united to him by faith, John vi. 57, "As the living Father hath sent me, and I live by the Father; so, he that eateth me, even he shall live by me." By Christ as Mediator, not as God only, as some have asserted; nor yet as man only, as the papists generally hold: but as Mediator, God and man, Acts xx. 28, "The church of God, which he hath purchased with his own blood." Heb. ix. 14, "Christ, who, through the eternal Spirit, offered himself without spot to God." The divine and human natures have their distinct actings, yet a joint operation, in his discharging the office of Mediator. This is illustrated by the similitude of a fiery sword, which at once cuts and burns: cutting it burns, and burning it cuts; the steel cuts, and the fire burns. Wherefore Christ, God-man, is the stock, whereof believers are the branches: and they are united to a whole Christ. They are united to him in his human nature, as being "members of his body, of his flesh, and of his bones," Eph. v. 30. And they are united to him in his divine nature; for so the apostle speaks of this union, Col. i. 27, "Christ in you, the hope of glory."—Those who are Christ's, have the Spirit of Christ, Rom. viii. 9; and by him they are united to the Father, and to the Holy Ghost; 1 John iv. 15, "Whosoever shall confess that Jesus is the Son of God, God dwelleth in him, and he in God." Faith, the bond of this union, receives a whole Christ, God-man, and so unites us to him as such.

Behold here, O believers, your high privilege. You were once branches of a degenerate stock, even as others: but you are, by grace, become branches of the true vine, John xv. 1. You are cut out of a dead and killing stock, and ingrafted in the last Adam, who was made a quickening spirit, 1 Cor. xv. 45. Your loss by the first Adam is made up, with great advantage, by your union with the second. Adam, at his best estate, was but a shrub, in comparison with Christ the tree of life. He was but a servant; Christ is the Son, the Heir, and Lord of all things, "the Lord from heaven." It cannot be denied, that grace was shown in the first covenant: but it is as far exceeded by the grace of the second covenant, as the twilight is by the light of the mid-day.

III. What branches are taken out of the natural stock, and grafted into this vine? *Answer.* These are the elect, and none other. They, and they only, are grafted into Christ; and consequently none but they are cut off from the killing stock. For them alone he intercedes, "That they may be one in him and his Father," John xvii. 9—23. Faith, the bond of this union, is given to none else; it is the faith of God's elect, Tit. i. 1. The Lord passes by many branches growing on the natural stock, and cuts off only here one, and there one, and grafts them into the true vine, according as free love hath determined. Often does he pitch upon the most unlikely branch, leaving the top boughs; passing by the mighty and the noble, and calling the weak, base, and despised, 1 Cor. i. 26, 27. Yea, he often leaves the fair and smooth, and takes the rugged and knotty; "and such were some of you, but ye are washed," &c. 1 Cor. vi. 11. If we inquire why so? We find no other reason but because they were chosen in him, Eph. i. 4; "predestinated to the adoption of children by Jesus Christ," ver. 5. Thus are they gathered together in Christ, while the rest are left growing on their natural stock, to be afterwards bound up in bundles for the fire. Therefore, to whomsoever the Gospel may come in vain, it will have a blessed effect on God's elect, Acts xiii. 48, "as many as were ordained to eternal life, believed." Where the Lord has much people, the gospel will have much success, sooner or later. Such as are to be saved, will be added to the mystical body of Christ.

IV. I am now to shew how the branches are cut off from the natural stock, the first Adam, and grafted into the true vine, the Lord Jesus Christ. Thanks to the Husbandman, not to the branch, that is cut off from its natural stock, and grafted into a new one. The sinner, in his coming off from the first stock, is passive, and neither can nor will come off from it of his own accord, but clings to it, till almighty power makes him to fall off, John vi. 44, "No man can come unto me, except the Father, which hath sent me, draw him." And chap. v. 40, "Ye will not come to me, that ye might have life." The ingrafted branches are " God's husbandry," 1 Cor. iii. 9, " The planting of the Lord," Isa. lxi. 3.—The ordinary means he makes use of, in this work, is the ministry of the word, 1 Cor. iii. 9, " We are labourers together with God." But the efficacy thereof is wholly from him, whatever the minister's parts or piety be, ver. 7, " Neither is he that planteth any thing, neither he that watereth ; but God that giveth the increase." The apostles preached to the Jews, yet the body of that people remained in infidelity, Rom. x. 16, " Who hath believed our report ?" Yea, Christ himself, who spoke as never man spoke, says concerning the success of his own ministry, "I have laboured in vain, I have spent my strength for nought," Isa. xlix. 4. The branches may be hacked by the preaching of the word ; but the stroke will never go through, till it is carried home by the omnipotent arm. However, God's ordinary way is, " by the foolishness of preaching to save them that believe," 1 Cor. i. 21.

The cutting of the branch from the natural stock, is performed by the pruning knife of the law, in the hand of the Spirit of God, Gal. ii. 19, " For I, through the law, am dead to the law." It is by the bond of the covenant of works, as I said before, that we are knit to our natural stock : therefore, as a wife, unwilling to be put away, pleads and hangs by the marriage tie; so do men by the covenant of works. They hold by it, like the man who held the ship with his hands ; and when one hand was cut off, held it with the other ; and when both were cut off, held it with his teeth. This will appear from a distinct view of the Lord's works on men, in bringing them off from the old stock ; which I offer in the following particulars :—

1. When the Spirit of the Lord comes to deal with a person, to bring him to Christ, he finds him in Laodicea's case, in a sound sleep of security, dreaming of heaven and the favour of God, though full of sin against the Holy One of Israel, Rev. iii. 17, " Thou knowest not that thou art wretched, and miserable, and poor, and blind, and naked." Therefore he darts in some beams of light into the dark soul ; and lets the man see that he is a lost man, if he turn not over a new leaf, and betake himself to a new course of life. Thus, by the Spirit of the Lord acting as a spirit of bondage, there is a criminal court erected in the man's breast ; where he is arraigned, accused, and condemned for breaking the law of God, " convicted of sin and judgment," John xvi. 8. And now he can no longer sleep securely in his former course of life. This is the first stroke which the branch gets, in order to cutting off.

2. Hereupon the man forsakes his former profane courses, his lying, swearing, Sabbath-breaking, stealing, and such like practices ; though they be dear to him as right eyes, he will rather quit them

than ruin his soul. The ship is likely to sink, and therefore he throws his goods overboard, that he himself may not perish. Now he begins to bless himself in his heart, and looks joyfully on his evidences for heaven; thinking himself a better servant to God than many others, Luke xviii. 11, "God, I thank thee, I am not as other men are, extortioners, unjust, adulterers," &c. But he soon gets another stroke with the axe of the law, shewing him that it is only he that doeth what is written in the law, that can be saved by it; and that his negative holiness is too scanty a covering from the storm of God's wrath. Thus, although his sins of commission only were heavy on him before, his sins of omission now crowd into his thoughts, attended with a train of law curses and vengeance. And each of the ten commandments discharges thunder-claps of wrath against him for his omission of required duties.

3. Upon this he turns to a positively holy course of life. He not only is not profane, but he performs religious duties: he prays, seeks the knowledge of the principles of religion, strictly observes the Lord's day, and, like Herod, does many things, and hears sermons gladly. In one word, there is a great conformity, in his outward conversation, to the letter of both tables of the law. There is a mighty change in the man, which his neighbours cannot miss taking notice of. Hence he is cheerfully admitted by the godly into their society, as a praying person; and can confer with them about religious matters, yea, and about soul exercise, which some are not acquainted with; and their good opinion of him confirms his good opinion of himself. This step in religion is fatal to many, who never get beyond it. But here the Lord gives the elect branch a farther stroke. Conscience flies in the man's face, for some wrong steps in his conversation, the neglect of some duty, or commission of some sin, which is a blot in his conversation; and then the flaming sword of the law appears again over his head, and the curse rings in his ears, for that he "continueth not in *all things* written in the law, to do them," Gal. iii. 10.

4. On this account, he is obliged to seek another remedy for his disease. He goes to God, confesses his sin, seeks the pardon of it, promising to watch against it for the time to come; and so finds ease, and thinks he may very well take it, seeing the scripture saith, "If we confess our sins, he is faithful and just to forgive us our sins," 1 John i. 9; not considering that he grasps at a privilege, which is theirs only who are grafted into Christ, and under the covenant of grace, and which the branches yet growing on the old stock cannot plead.—And here sometimes there are formal and express vows made against such and such sins, and binding to such and

such duties. Thus many go on all their days, knowing no other religion, than to perform duties, and to confess, and pray for pardon of that wherein they fail, promising themselves eternal happiness, though they are utter strangers to Christ. Here many elect ones have been cast down wounded, and many reprobates have been slain, while the wounds of neither of them have been deep enough to cut them off from their natural stock. But the Spirit of the Lord gives yet a deeper stroke to the branch which is to be cut off, shewing him, that, as yet, he is but an outside saint, and discovering to him the filthy lusts lodged in his heart, which he took no notice of before, Rom. vii. 9, "When the commandment came, sin revived, and I died." Then he sees his heart to be full of sinful lusts, covetousness, pride, malice, filthiness and the like. Now, as soon as the door of the chambers of his imagery is thus opened to him, and he sees what they do there in the dark, his outside religion is blown up as insufficient; and he learns a new lesson in religion, namely, "That he is not a Jew, who is one outwardly," Rom. ii. 28.

5. Upon this he goes farther, even to inside religion; sets to work more vigorously than ever, mourns over the evils of his heart, and strives to bear down the weeds which he finds growing in that neglected garden. He labours to curb his pride and passion, and to banish speculative impurities; prays more fervently, hears attentively, and strives to get his heart affected in every religious duty he performs; and thus he comes to think himself, not only an outside, but an inside Christian.—Wonder not at this, for there is nothing in it beyond the power of nature, or what one may attain to under a vigorous influence of the covenant of works; therefore another yet deeper stroke is given. The law charges home on the man's conscience, that he was a transgressor from the womb; that he came into the world a guilty creature; and that in the time of his ignorance, and even since his eyes were opened, he has been guilty of many actual sins, either altogether overlooked by him or not sufficiently mourned over, for spiritual sores, not healed by the blood of Christ, but skinned over some other way, so as to be easily irritated, and soon to break out again; therefore the law takes him by the throat, saying, "Pay what thou owest."

6. Then the sinner says in his heart, "Have patience with me, and I will pay thee all;" and so falls to work to pacify an offended God, and to atone for those sins. He renews his repentance, such as it is; bears patiently the afflictions laid upon him; yea, he afflicts himself, denies himself the use of his lawful comforts, sighs deeply mourns bitterly, cries with tears for a pardon, till he has wrought up his heart to a conceit of having obtained it: having thus done

penance for what is past, he resolves to be a good servant to God, and to hold on in outward and inward obedience, for the time to come. —But the stroke must go nearer the heart yet, ere the branch falls off. The Lord discovers to him, in the glass of the law, how he sinneth in all he does, even when he does the best he can; and therefore the dreadful sound returns to his ears, Gal. iii. 10, "Cursed is every one that continueth not in all things," &c. "When ye fasted and mourned," saith the Lord, "did ye at all fast unto me, even to me?" Will muddy water make clean clothes? Will you satisfy for one sin with another? Did not your thoughts wander in such a duty? Were not your affections flat in another? Did not your heart give a sinful look to such an idol? And did it not rise in a fit of impatience under such an affliction? "Should I accept this of your hands? Cursed be the deceiver, which sacrificeth to the Lord a corrupt thing," Mal. i. 13, 14. And thus he becomes so far broken off, that he sees he is not able to satisfy the demands of the law.

7. Hence, like a broken man, who finds he is not able to pay all his debt, he goes about to compound with his creditor. And, being in pursuit of ease and comfort, he does what he can to fulfil the law; and wherein he fails, he trusts that God will accept the will for the deed. Thus doing his duty, and having a will to do better, he cheats himself into persuasion of the goodness of his state: and hereby thousands are ruined. But the elect get another stroke, which loosens their hold in this case. The doctrine of the law is borne in on their consciences, demonstrating to them, that exact and perfect obedience is required by it, under pain of the curse; and that it is doing, and not wishing to do, which will avail. Wishing to do better will not answer the law's demands; and therefore the curse sounds again, "Cursed is every one that continueth not— to do them;" that is, actually to do them. In vain is wishing then.

3. Being broken off from all hopes of compounding with the law, he falls to borrowing. He sees that all he can do to obey the law, and all his desires to be and to do better, will not save his soul: therefore he goes to Christ, entreating, that his righteousness may make up what is wanting in his own, and cover all the defects of his doings and sufferings; that so God, for Christ's sake, may accept them, and thereupon be reconciled. Thus doing what he can to fulfil the law, and looking to Christ to make up all his defects, he comes at length to sleep securely again. Many persons are ruined this way. This was the error of the Galatians, which Paul, in his epistle to them, disputes against. But the Spirit of God breaks off the sinner from this hold also, by bringing home to his conscience that great truth, Gal. iii. 12, "The law is not of faith, but the man

that doeth them shall live in them." There is no mixing of the law and faith in this business; the sinner must hold by one of them, and let the other go. The way of the law, and the way of faith, are so far different, that it is not possible for a sinner to walk in the one, unless he comes off from the other: and if he be for doing, he must do all alone; Christ will not do a part for him, if he do not all. A garment pieced up of sundry sorts of righteousness, is not a garment meet for the court of heaven. Thus the man is like one in a dream, who thought he was eating, but being awakened by a stroke, behold his soul is faint; his heart sinks in him like a stone, while he finds that he can neither bear his burden himself alone, nor can he get help under it.

9. What can he do who must needs pay, and yet has not enough of his own to bring him out of debt; nor can borrow so much, and is ashamed to beg?—What can such a one do, I say, but sell himself, as the man under the law, that was, become poor? Lev. xxv. 47. Therefore the sinner, beat off from so many holds, attempts to make a bargain with Christ, and to sell himself to the Son of God, if I may so speak, solemnly promising and vowing, that he will be a servant to Christ, as long as he lives, if he will save his soul. And here, the sinner often makes a personal covenant with Christ, resigning himself to him on these terms; yea, and takes the sacrament, to make the bargain sure. Hereupon the man's great care is, how to obey Christ, keep his commandments, and so fulfil his bargain. In this the soul finds a false, unsound peace, for a while; till the Spirit of the Lord gives another stroke, to cut off the man from this refuge of lies likewise. And that happens in this manner: when he fails of the duties he engaged to perform, and falls again into the sin he covenanted against, it is powerfully carried home on his conscience, that his covenant is broken; so all his comfort goes, and terrors afresh seize on his soul, as one that has broken covenant with Christ. Commonly the man to help himself, renews his covenant, but breaks it again as before. And how is it possible it should be otherwise, seeing he is still upon the old stock? Thus the work of many, all their days, as to their souls, is nothing but a making and breaking such covenants, over and over again.

Objection. Some perhaps will say, " Who liveth, and sinneth not? Who is there that faileth not of the duties he has engaged to? If you reject this way as unsound, who then can be saved?" *Answer.* True believers will be saved, namely, all who do by faith take hold of God's covenant. But this kind of covenant is men's own covenant, devised of their own heart; not God's covenant, revealed in the gospel of his grace: and the making of it is nothing else but the making of a covenant of works with Christ, confounding the law and the Gospel; a covenant he will never subscribe to, though we should sign it with our heart's blood. Rom. iv. 14, 16, "For if they which are of the law be heirs, faith is made void, and the promise made of none effect.—Therefore it is of faith, that it might be by grace, to the end the promise might be sure to all the seed." Chap. xi. 6, "And if by grace, then is it no more of works, otherwise grace is no more grace. But if it be of works, then is it no more grace, otherwise work is no more work." God's covenant is everlasting; once in and never out of it again; and the mercies of it are sure mercies, Isa. lv. 3. But that covenant of yours is a tottering covenant, never sure, but broken every day. It is a mere servile covenant, giving Christ service for salvation; but God's covenant is a filial covenant, in which the sinner takes Christ, and his salvation freely offered, and so becomes a son, John i. 12, "But as many as received him, to them gave he power to become the sons of God:" and being become a son, he serves his Father, not that the inheritance may become his, but because it is his, through Jesus Christ. See Gal. iv. 24, and onward. To enter into that false covenant, is to buy from Christ with money; but to take hold of God's covenant, is to buy of him without money and without price, Isa. lv. 1, that is to say, to beg of him. In that covenant men work for life; in God's covenant they come to Christ for life, and work from life. When a person under that covenant fails in his duty, all is gone; the covenant must be made over again. But under God's covenant, although the man fail in his duty, and for his failure falls under the discipline of the covenant, and lies under the weight of it, till such time as he has recourse anew to the blood of Christ for pardon, and renew his repentance; yet all that he trusted to, for life and salvation, namely, the righteousness of Christ, still stands entire, and the covenant remains firm. See Rom. vii. 24, 25; and chap. viii. 1.

Now, though some men spend their lives in making and breaking such covenants of their own, the terror on the breaking of them becoming weaker and weaker, by degrees, till at last it creates them little or no uneasiness; yet the man, in whom the good work is carried on, till it be accomplished in cutting him off from the old stock, finds these covenants to be as rotten cords, broken at every touch; and the terror of God being thereupon redoubled on his spirit and, the waters at every turn getting in unto his very soul, he is obliged to cease from catching hold of such covenants and to seek help some other way.

10. Therefore the man comes at length to beg at Christ's door for

mercy; but yet he is a proud beggar, standing on his personal worth. For, as the papists have Mediators to plead for them, with the one only Mediator, so the branches of the old stock have always something to produce, which they think may commend them to Christ, and engage him to take their cause in hand. They cannot think of coming to the spiritual market, without money in their hand. They are like persons who have once had an estate of their own, but are reduced to extreme poverty, and forced to beg. When they come to beg, they still remember their former character; and though they have lost their substance: yet they retain much of their former spirit: therefore they cannot think that they ought to be treated as ordinary beggars, but deserve a particular regard; and, if that be not given them, their spirits rise against him to whom they address themselves for a supply. Thus God gives the unhumbled sinner many common mercies, and shuts him not up in the pit according to his deserving; but all this is nothing in his eyes. He must be set down at the children's table, otherwise he reckons himself hardly dealt with, and wronged: for he is not yet brought so low, as to think God may be justified when he speaks against him, and clear from all iniquity, when he judgeth him according to his real demerit, Psalm li. 4. He thinks, perhaps, that, even before he was enlightened, he was better than many others; he considers his reformation of life, his repentance, the grief and tears which his sin has cost him, his earnest desires after Christ, his prayers and wrestlings for mercy; and uses all these now as bribes for mercy, laying no small weight upon them in his addresses to the throne of grace. But here the Spirit of the Lord shoots his arrows quickly into the man's heart, whereby his confidence in these things is sunk and destroyed; and, instead of thinking himself better than many, he is made to see himself worse than any. The faults in his reformation of life are discovered; his repentance appears to him no better than the repentance of Judas; his tears like Esau's, and his desires after Christ to be selfish and loathsome, like those who sought Christ because of the loaves, John vi. 26. His answer from God seems now to be, Away, proud beggar, "How shall I put thee among the children?" He seems to look sternly on him, for his slighting of Jesus Christ by unbelief, which is a sin he scarcely discerned before. But now at length he beholds it in its crimson colours, and is pierced to the heart, as with a thousand darts, while he sees how he has been going on blindly, sinning against the remedy of sin, and, in the whole course of his life, trampling on the blood of the Son of God. And now he is, in his own eyes, the miserable object of law vengeance, yea, and gospel vengeance too.

11. The man being thus far humbled, will no more plead, "he is worthy for whom Christ should do this thing;" but, on the contrary, looks on himself as unworthy of Christ, and unworthy of the favour of God. We may compare him, in this case, to the young man who followed Christ, having a linen cloth cast about his naked body; who, when the young men laid hold of him, left the linen cloth, and fled from them naked," Mark xiv. 51, 52. Even so the man had been following Christ, in the thin and cold garment of his own personal worthiness: but by it, even by it, which he so much trusted to, the law catches hold of him, to make him prisoner; and then he is fain to leave it, and flees away naked—yet not to Christ, but from him. If you now tell him he is welcome to Christ, if he will come to him; he is apt to say, Can such a vile and unworthy wretch as I, be welcome to the holy Jesus? If a plaster be applied to his wounded soul, it will not stick. He says, "depart from me, for I am a sinful man, O Lord," Luke v. 8. No man needs speak to him of his repentance, for his comfort; he can quickly espy such faults in it as makes it naught: nor of his tears; for he is assured they have never come into the Lord's bottle. He disputes himself away from Christ; and concludes, now that he has been such a slighter of Christ, and is such an unholy and vile creature, that he cannot, he will not, he ought not to come to Christ; and that he must either be in better case, or else he will never believe. Hence he now makes the strongest efforts to amend what was amiss in his way before: he prays more earnestly than ever, mourns more bitterly, strives against sin in heart and life more vigorously, and watches more diligently, if by any means he may at length be fit to come to Christ. One would think the man is well humbled now: but, ah! deep pride lurks under the veil of this seeming humility; like a kindly branch of the old stock, he adheres still, and will not submit to the righteousness of God, Rom. x. 3. He will not come to the market of free grace, without money. He is bidden to the marriage of the King's Son, where the bridegroom himself furnishes all the guests with wedding garments, stripping them of their own: but he will not come, because he wants a wedding garment; although he is very busy in making one ready. This is sad work; and therefore he must have a deeper stroke yet, else he is ruined. This stroke is given him with the axe of the law, in its irritating power. Thus the law, girding the soul with cords of death, and holding it in with the rigorous commands of obedience, under the pain of the curse; and God, in his holy and wise conduct, withdrawing his restraining grace, corruption is irritated, lusts become violent; and the more they are striven against the more they

rage, like a furious horse checked with the bit. Then corruptions set up their heads, which he never saw in himself before. Here ofttimes, atheism, blashpemy, and, in one word, horrible things concerning God, terrible thoughts concerning the faith, arise in his breast; so that his heart is a very hell within him. Thus, while he is sweeping the house of his heart, not yet watered with gospel grace, those corruptions which lay quiet before, in neglected corners, fly up and down in it like dust. He is as one who is mending the bank of a river, and while he is repairing breaches in it, and strengthening every part of it, a mighty flood comes down, and overturns his works, and drives all away before it, both that which was newly laid, and what was laid before. Read Rom. vii. 8—13. This is a stroke which goes to the heart : and by it, his hope of making himself more fit to come to Christ, is cut off.

12. Now the time is come, when the man, between hope and despair, resolves to go to Christ as he is; and therefore, like a dying man, stretching himself just before his breath goes out, he rallies the broken forces of his soul, tries to believe, and in some sort lays hold on Jesus Christ. And now the branch hangs on the old stock by one single tack of a natural faith, produced by the natural vigour of one's own spirit, under a most pressing necessity, Psalm lxxviii. 34, 35, " When he slew them, then they sought him, and they returned and inquired early after God. And they remembered that God was their rock, and the high God their Redeemer." Hos. viii. 2, " Israel shall cry unto me, My God, we know thee." But the Lord, never failing to perfect his work, fetches yet another stroke, whereby the branch falls quite off. The Spirit of God convincingly discovers to the sinner his utter inability to do any thing that is good, and so he dieth, Rom. vii. 9. That voice powerfully strikes through his soul, " How can ye believe ?" John v. 44. Thou canst no more believe, than thou canst reach up thine hand to heaven, and bring Christ down from thence. Thus at length he sees, that he can neither help himself by working, nor by believing ; and having no more to hang by on the old stock, he therefore falls off. While he is distressed thus, seeing himself likely to be swept away with the flood of God's wrath, and yet unable so much as to stretch forth a hand to lay hold of a twig of the tree of life, growing on the bank of the river, he is taken up, and ingrafted in the true vine, the Lord Jesus Christ giving him the Spirit of faith.

By what has been said upon this head, I design not to rack or distress tender consciences; for though there are but few such at this day, yet God forbid that I should offend any of Christ's little ones. But, alas ! a dead sleep is fallen upon this generation, they will not be awakened, let us go ever so near to the quick: therefore I fear that there is another sort of awakening abiding this sermon-proof generation, which shall make the ears of them that hear it tingle. However, I would not have this to be looked upon as the sovereign God's stinted method of breaking off sinners from the old stock. But this I maintain as a certain truth, that all who are in Christ have been broken off from all these several confidences; and that they who were never broken off from them, are yet in their natural stock. Nevertheless, if the house be pulled down, and the old foundation razed, it is much the same whether it was taken down stone by stone, or whether it was undermined, and all fell down together.

Now it is that the branch is ingrafted in Jesus Christ. And as the law, in the hand of the Spirit of God, was the instrument to cut off the branch from the natural stock; so the Gospel, in the hand of the same Spirit, is the instrument used for ingrafting it into the supernatural stock, 1 John i. 3. "That which we have seen and heard, declare we unto you, that ye also may have fellowship with us; and truly our fellowship is with the Father, and with his Son Jesus Christ." See Isaiah lxi. 1—3. The Gospel is the silver cord let down from heaven, to draw perishing sinners to land. And though the preaching of the law prepares the way of the Lord; yet it is in the word of the Gospel that Christ and a sinner meet. Now, as in the natural grafting, the branch being taken up is put into the stock, and being put into it, becomes one with it, so that they are united; even so in the spiritual ingrafting, Christ apprehends the sinner, and the sinner, being apprehended of Christ, apprehends him, and so they become one, Phil. iii. 12.

First, Christ apprehends the sinner by his Spirit, and draws him to himself, 1 Cor. xii. 13, "For by one Spirit we are all baptized into one body." The same Spirit which is in the Mediator himself, he communicates to his elect in due time, never to depart from them, but to abide in them as a principle of life. The soul is now in the hands of the Lord of life, and possessed by the Spirit of life; how can it then but live? The man gets a ravishing sight of Christ's excellence in the glass of the gospel: he sees him a full, suitable, and willing Saviour; and gets a heart to take him for and instead of all. The Spirit of faith furnishes him feet to come to Christ, and hands to receive him. What by nature he could not do, by grace he can, the Holy Spirit working in him the work of faith with power.

Secondly, The sinner, thus apprehended, apprehends Christ by faith, and is one with the blessed stock, Eph. iii. 17, "That Christ may dwell in your hearts by faith." The soul that before tried many ways of escape, but all in vain, now looks with the eye of faith, which proves the healing look. As Aaron's rod, laid up in the tabernacle, budded, and brought forth buds, Numb. xvii. 8; so the dead breach, apprehended by the Lord of life, put into, and bound up with the glorious quickening stock, by the Spirit of life buds forth in actual believing on Jesus Christ, whereby this union is completed. "We, having the same Spirit of faith—believe," 2 Cor. iv. 13. Thus the stock and the graft are united, Christ and the Christian are married, faith being the soul's consent to the spiritual marriage covenant, which as it is proposed in the gospel to mankind-sinners indefinitely, so it is demonstrated, attested, and brought home to the man in particular, by the Holy Spirit: and so he, being joined to the Lord, is one Spirit with him. Hereby a believer lives in and for Christ, and Christ lives in and for the believer, Gal. ii. 20, "I am crucified with Christ: nevertheless, I live; yet not I, but Christ liveth in me." Hos. iii. 3, "Thou shalt not be for another man, so will I also be for thee." The bonds, then, of this blessed union are, the Spirit on Christ's part, and faith on the believer's part.

Now both the souls and bodies of believers are united to Christ. "He that is joined to the Lord is one Spirit," 1 Cor. vi. 17. The very bodies of believers have this honour put upon them, that they are "the temple of the Holy Ghost," ver. 19, and "the members of Christ," ver. 15. When they sleep in the dust, they sleep in Jesus, 1 Thess. iv. 14; and it is in virtue of this union they shall be raised up out of the dust again, Rom. viii. 11, "He shall quicken your mortal bodies, by his Spirit that dwelleth in you." In token of this mystical union, the church of believers is called by the name of her Head and Husband, 1 Cor. xii. 12, "For as the body is one, and hath many members—so also is Christ."

USE. From what is said, we may draw the following inferences:

1. The preaching of the law is most necessary. He that would ingraft, must needs use the pruning-knife.—Sinners have many contrivances to keep them from Christ; many things by which they keep their hold of the natural stock; therefore they have need to be closely pursued, and hunted out of their skulking holes, and refuges of lies.

2. Yet it is the Gospel that crowns the work: "The law makes nothing perfect." The law lays open the wound, but it is the Gospel that heals it. The law "strips a man, wounds him and leaves him half dead:" the Gospel "binds up his wounds, pouring in wine and oil," to heal them. By the law we are broken off, but it is by the Gospel we are taken up and implanted in Christ.

3. "If any man have not the Spirit of Christ he is none of his," Rom. viii. 9. We are told of a monster in nature, having two bodies differently animated, as appeared from contrary affections at one and the same time; but so united, that they were served with the self-same legs. Even so, however men may cleave to Christ, "call themselves of the holy city, and stay themselves upon the God of Israel," Isa xlviii. 2, and may be bound up as branches in him, John xv. 2, by the outward ties of sacraments; yet if the Spirit that dwells in Christ, dwell not in them, they are not one with him. There is a great difference between adhesion and ingrafting. The ivy clasps and twists itself about the oak, but it is not one with it, for it still grows on its own root: so, to allude to Isa. iv. 1, many professors "take hold" of Christ, "and eat their own bread, and wear their own apparel, only they are called by his name." They stay themselves upon him, but grow upon their own root: they take them to support their hopes, but their delights are elsewhere.

4. The union between Christ and his mystical members is firm and indissoluble. Were it so that the believer only apprehended Christ, but Christ apprehended not him, we could promise little as the stability of such a union; it might quickly be dissolved: but as the believer apprehends Christ by faith, so Christ apprehends him by his Spirit, and none shall pluck him out of his hand.—Did the child only keep hold of the nurse, it might at length grow weary, and let go its hold, and so fall away: but if she have her arms about the child, it is in no hazard of falling away, even though it be not actually holding by her. So, whatever sinful intermissions may happen in the exercise of faith; yet the union remains sure, by reason of the constant indwelling of the spirit. Blessed Jesus! "All his saints are in thy hand," Deut. xxxiii. 3. It is observed by some that the word Abba, is the same whether you read it forward or backward: whatever the believer's case be, the Lord is still to him, Abba, Father.

5. They have an unsafe hold of Christ, whom he has not apprehended by his Spirit. There are many half marriages here, where the soul apprehends Christ, but is not apprehended of him. Hence, many fall away, and never rise again; they let go their hold of Christ; and when that is gone, all is gone. These are "the branches in Christ that bear not fruit, which the husbandman taketh away," John xv. 2. *Question.* How can that be? *Answer.* These branches are set in the stock by a profession, or an unsound hypocritical faith; they are bound up with it, in the external use of the sacraments; but the stock and they are never knit; therefore

they cannot bear fruit. And they need not be cut off, nor broken off; they are by the Husbandman only taken away; or, as the word primarily signifies, lifted up, and so taken away, because there is nothing to hold them; they are indeed bound up with the stock, but were never united to it.

Question. How shall I know if I am apprehended of Christ? *Answer.* You may be satisfied in this inquiry, if you consider and apply these two things:

1. When Christ apprehends a man by his Spirit, he is so drawn, that he comes away to Christ, with his whole heart: for true believing is believing with all the heart, Acts viii. 37. Our Lord's followers are like those who followed Saul at first, men whose hearts God has touched, 1 Sam. x. 26. When the Spirit pours in overcoming grace, they pour out their hearts like water before him, Psalm lxii. 8. They flow unto him like a river, Isa. ii. 2, "All nations shall flow unto it," namely, to the "mountain of the Lord's house." It denotes not only the abundance of converts, but the disposition of their souls in coming to Christ; they come heartily and freely, as drawn with loving-kindness, Jer. xxxi. 3, "Thy people shall be willing in the day of thy power," Psalm cx. 3, that is, free, ready, open-hearted, giving themselves to thee as free-will offering. When the bridegroom has the bride's heart, it is a right marriage: but some give their hand to Christ, who give him not their heart. They that are only driven to Christ by terror, will surely leave him again when that terror is gone. Terror may break a heart of stone, but the pieces into which it is broken still continue to be stone: terrors cannot soften it into a heart of flesh. Yet terrors may begin the work which love crowns. The strong wind, and the earthquake, and the fire going before; the still small voice, in which the Lord is, may come after them. When the blessed Jesus is seeking sinners to match with him, they are bold and perverse: they will not speak with him, till he has wounded them, made them captives, and bound them with the cords of death. When this is done, then it is that he comes to them, and wins their hearts. The Lord tells us, Hos. ii. 16—20, that is chosen Israel shall be married unto himself. But how will the bride's consent be won? Why, in the first place, he will bring her into the wilderness, as he did the people when he brought them out of Egypt, ver. 14. There she will be hardly dealt with, scorched with thirst, and bitten of serpents: and then he will speak comfortably to her; or, as the expression is, he will speak unto her heart. The sinner is first driven, and then drawn unto Christ. It is with the soul as with Noah's dove, she was forced back again to the ark, because she

could find nothing else to rest upon: but when she returned, she would have rested on the outside of it, if Noah had not " put forth his hand and pulled her in," Gen. viii. 9. The Lord sends his avenger of blood in pursuit of the criminal, who with a sad heart leaves his own city, and with tears in his eyes parts with his old acquaintances, because he dare not stay with them, and he flees for his life to the city of refuge. This is not all his choice, it is forced work; necessity has now law. But when he comes to the gates, and sees the beauty of the place, the excellency and loveliness of it charm him; and then he enters it with heart and good-will, saying, "This is my rest, and here I will stay;" and, as one said in another case, " I had perished, unless I had perished."

2. When Christ apprehends a soul, the heart is disengaged from, and turned against sin. As in cutting off the branch from the old stock, the great idol self is brought down, the man is powerfully taught to deny himself; so, in apprehending the sinner by the Spirit, that union is dissolved which was between the man and his lusts, while he was in the flesh, as the apostle expresses it, Rom. vii. 5. His heart is loosened from them, though formerly as dear to him as the members of his body; as his eyes, legs, or arms; and, instead of taking pleasure in them as before, he longs to be rid of them. When the Lord Jesus comes to a soul, in the day of converting grace, he finds it like Jerusalem, in the day of her nativity, Ezek. xvi. 4, drawing its fulsome nourishment and satisfaction from its lusts: but he cuts off this communication, that he may impart to the soul his own consolations, and give it rest in himself. And thus the Lord wounds the head and heart of sin, and the soul comes to him, saying, " Surely our fathers have inherited lies, vanity, and things wherein there is no profit," Jer. xvi. 19.

V. I proceed to speak of the benefits flowing to true believers from their union with Christ. The chief of the particular benefits which believers have by it, are justification, peace, adoption, sanctification, growth in grace, fruitfulness in good works, acceptance of these works, establishment in the state of grace, support and a special conduct of providence about them. As for communion with Christ, it is such a benefit, as being the immediate consequence of union with him, comprehends all the rest as mediate ones. For as the branch, immediately upon its union with the stock, has communion with the stock in all that is in it; so the believer, uniting with Christ, has communion with him; in which he launches forth into an ocean of happiness, is led into a paradise of pleasures, and has a saving interest in the treasure hid in the field of the Gospel, the unsearchable riches of Christ. As soon as the believer is united to Christ, Christ himself, in whom all fulness dwells, is his, Cant. iii. 16, "My beloved is mine, and I am his." And "how shall he not with him freely give us all things?" Rom. viii. 32, "Whether Paul, or Apollos, or Cephas, or the world, or life, or death, or things present, or things to come, all are yours," 1 Cor. iii. 22. This communion with Christ is the great comprehensive blessing necessarily flowing from our union with him. Let us now consider the particular benefits flowing from it before mentioned.

The first particular benefit that a sinner has by his union with Christ, is justification; for, being united to Christ, he has communion with him in his righteousness, 1 Cor. i. 30, "But of him are ye in Christ Jesus, who of God is made unto us wisdom and righteousness." He stands no more condemned, but justified before God, as being in Christ, Rom. viii. 1, "There is therefore now no condemnation to them which are in Christ Jesus." The branches hereof are, pardon of sin, and personal acceptance.

1. His sins are pardoned, the guilt of them is removed. The bond obliging him to pay his debt is cancelled. God the Father takes the pen, dips it in the blood of his Son, crosses the sinner's accounts, and blots them out of his debt-book. The sinner out of Christ is bound over to the wrath of God; he is under an obligation in law to go to the prison of hell, and there to lie till he has paid the utmost farthing. This arises from the terrible sanction with which the law is guarded, which is no less than death, Gen. ii. 17. So that the sinner, passing the bounds assigned him, is as Shimei in another case, a man of death, 1 Kings ii. 42. But now, being united to Christ, God saith, "Deliver him from going down to the pit; I have found a ransom," Job xxxiii. 24, The sentence of condemnation is reversed, the believer is absolved, and set beyond the reach of the condemning law. His sins, which were set before the Lord, Psalm xc. 8, so that they could not be hid, God now takes and casts them all behind his back, Isa. xxxviii. 17. Yea, he casts them into the depths of the sea, Micah vii. 19. What falls into a brook may be got up again, but what is cast into the sea cannot be recovered. But there are some shallow places in the sea: true, but their sins are not cast in there, but into the depths of the sea; and the depths of the sea are devouring depths, from whence they shall never come forth again. But what if they do not sink? He will cast them in with force, so that they shall go to the ground, and sink as lead in the mighty waters of the Redeemer's blood. They are not only forgiven, but forgotten, Jer. xxxi. 34, "I will forgive their iniquity, and I will remember their sin no more." And

though their after-sins do in themselves deserve eternal wrath, and do actually make them liable to temporal strokes, and fatherly chastisements, according to the tenor of the covenant of grace, Psalm lxxxix. 30—33, yet they can never be actually liable to eternal wrath, or the curse of the law; for they are dead to the law in Christ, Rom. vii. 4. They can never fall away from their union with Christ; neither can they be in Christ, and yet under condemnation at the same time, Rom. viii. 1, "There is therefore now no condemnation to them which are in Christ Jesus." This is an inference drawn from that doctrine of the believer's being dead to the law, set forth by the apostle, chap. vii. 1—6; as is clear from the second, third, and fourth verses of this eighth chapter. In this respect the justified man is the blessed man, unto whom the Lord imputeth not iniquity, Psalm xxxii. 2; as one who has no design to charge a debt on another, sets it not down in his account-book.

2. The believer is accepted as righteous in God's sight, 2 Cor. v. 21. For he is "found in Christ, not having his own righteousness, but that which is through the faith of Christ, the righteousness which is of God by faith," Phil. iii. 9. He could never be accepted of God, as righteous, upon the account of his own righteousness; because, at best, it is but imperfect; and all righteousness, properly so called, which can abide a trial before the throne of God, is perfect. The very name of it implies perfection: for unless a work is perfectly conformable to the law, it is not right, but wrong; and so cannot make a man righteous before God, whose judgment is according to truth. Yet if justice demand a righteousness of one that is in Christ, upon which he may be accounted righteous before the Lord, "Surely shall" such a "one say, In the Lord have I righteousness," Isa. xlv. 24. The law is fulfilled, its commands are obeyed, its sanction is satisfied. The believer's surety has paid the debt. It was exacted, and he answered for it.

Thus the person united to Christ is justified. You may conceive of the whole proceeding herein, in this manner. The avenger of blood pursuing the criminal, Christ, as the Saviour of lost sinners, doth by the Spirit apprehend him, and draw him to himself; and he, by faith, lays hold on Christ: so the Lord our righteousness, and the unrighteous creature, unite. From this union with Christ results a communion with him in his unsearchable riches, and consequently in his righteousness, that white raiment which he has for clothing of the naked, Rev. iii. 18. Thus the righteousness of Christ becomes his; and because it is by his unquestionable title, it is imputed to him; it is reckoned his in the judgment of God, which is always according to truth. And so the believing sinner, having a righteousness which fully answers the demands of the law, he is pardoned and accepted as righteous. See Isa. xlv. 22—24; Rom. iii. 24; and chap. v. 1. Now he is a free man. Who shall lay any thing to the charge of those whom God justifieth? Can justice lay any thing to their charge? No; for it is satisfied. Can the law? No; for it has obtained all its demands on them in Jesus Christ, Gal. iii. 20, "I am crucified with Christ." What can the law require more, after it has wounded their head, poured in wrath in full measure into their soul, and cut off their life, and brought it into the dust of death, by doing all this to Jesus Christ, who is their head, Eph. i. 22; their soul, Acts ii. 25—27; and their life, Col. iii. 4? What is become of the sinner's own handwriting, which would prove the debt upon him? Christ has blotted it out, Col. ii. 14. But it may be, justice may get its eye upon it again. No; he took it out of the way. But O that it had been torn in pieces! may the sinner say. Yea, so it is; the nails that pierced Christ's hands and feet are driven through it; he nailed it. But what if the torn in pieces be set together again? They cannot be; for he nailed it to his cross, and his cross was buried with him, and will never rise again, seeing Christ dieth no more. Where is the face-covering that was upon the condemned man? Christ has destroyed it, Isa. xxv. 7. Where is death, that stood before the sinner with a grim face, and an open mouth, ready to devour him? Christ has swallowd it up in victory, ver. 8, Glory, glory, glory to him that thus "loved us, and washed us from our sins in his own blood."

The second benefit flowing from the same spring of union with Christ, and coming by the way of justification, is peace; peace with God, and peace of conscience, according to the measure of the sense the justified have of their peace with God, Rom. v. 1. "Therefore being justified by faith, we have peace with God." Chap. xiv. 17, "For the kingdom of God is not meat and drink, but righteousness and peace, and joy in the Holy Ghost." Whereas God was their enemy before, now he is reconciled to them in Christ: they are in a covenant of peace with him; and, as Abraham was, so are they the friends of God. He is well pleased with them in his beloved Son. His word, which spoke terror to them formerly, now speaks peace, if they rightly understand the language. And there is love in all dispensations towards them, which makes all work together for their good. Their consciences are purged of that guilt and filthiness which lay upon them: his conscience-purifying blood streams through their souls, by virtue of their union with him, Heb. ix. 14, "How much more shall the blood of Christ—purge your conscience from dead works to serve the living God!" The bonds laid on their consciences by the Spirit of God, acting as the Spirit of bondage, are taken off, never more to be laid on, Rom. viii. 5, "For ye have not received the Spirit of bondage again to fear." Hereby the conscience is quieted, as soon as the soul becomes conscious of the application of that blood; which falls out sooner or later, according to the measure of faith, and as the only wise God sees meet to time it. Unbelievers may have troubled consciences, which they may get quieted again: but, alas! their consciences become peaceable before they become pure; so their peace is but the seed of greater horror and confusion. Carelessness may give ease for a while to a sick conscience; men neglecting its wounds, they close again of their accord, before the impure matter is removed. Many bury their guilt in the grave of an ill memory: conscience smarts a little; at length the man forgets his sin, and there is an end of it; but that is only an ease before death. Business, or the affairs of life, often give ease in this case. When Cain is banished from the presence of the Lord, he falls a-building of cities. When the evil spirit came upon Saul, he calls not for his Bible, nor for the priests to converse with him about his case; but for music, to play it away. So many, when their consciences begin to be uneasy, they fill their heads and hands with business, to divert themselves, and to regain ease at any rate. Yea, some will sin contrary to their convictions, and so do get some ease to their consciences, as Hazael gave ease to his master by stifling him. Again the performance of duties may give some ease to disqutied consciences; and this is all which legal professors have recourse to for quieting their consciences. When conscience is wounded they will pray, confess, mourn, and resolve to do so no more: and so they become whole again, without an application of the blood of Christ by faith. But they whose consciences are rightly quieted, come for peace and purification to the blood of sprinkling. Sin leaves a sting behind it, which one time or other will create them no little pain.

Elihu shews us both the case and cure, Job xxxiii.—Behold the case which a man may be in, whom God has thoughts of love to. He darts convictions into his conscience; and makes them stick so fast, that he cannot rid himself of them, ver. 16, " He openeth the ears of men, and sealeth their instruction. His very body sickens, ver. 19, " He is chastened also with pain upon his bed, and the multitude of his bones with strong pain " He loseth his appetite, ver. 20, " His life abhorreth bread, and his soul dainty meat." His body pines away, so that there is nothing on him but skin and bone," ver. 21, " His flesh is consumed away, that it cannot be seen, and his bones that were not seen stick out." Though he is not prepared for death, he has no hope of life, ver. 22, "His soul draweth near unto the grave, and" which is the height of his misery, " his life to the destroyers ;" he is looking every moment when devils, these destroyers, Rev. ix. 11, these murderers, or manslayers, John viii. 44, will come and carry away his soul to hell. O dreadful case? Is there any hope for such? Yes, there is hope. God will " keep back his soul from the pit," Job xxxiii. 18, although he bring him forward to the brink of it. Now, see how the sick man is cured. The physician's art cannot prevail here: the disease lies more inward than his medicines can reach. It is soul trouble that has brought the body into this disorder; and therefore the remedies must be applied to the sick man's soul and conscience. The physician for this case, must be a spiritual Physician; the remedies must be spiritual, a righteousness, a ransom, an atonement. Upon the application of these, the soul is cured, the conscience is quieted: and the body recovers, ver. 23—26, " If there be a messenger with him, an interpreter, one among a thousand, to show unto man his uprightness: then he is gracious unto him, and saith, Deliver him from going down into the pit, I have found a ransom. His flesh shall be fresher than a child's, he shall return to the days of his youth. He shall pray unto God, and he shall be favourable unto him, and he shall see his face with joy." The proper physician for this patient is a messenger, an interpreter, ver. 23, that is, as some expositors, not without ground, understand it, the great physician, Jesus Christ, whom Job had called his Redeemer, chap. xix. 25. He is a messenger, the " messenger of the covenant of peace," Mal. iii. 1, who comes seasonably to the sick man. He is an interpreter, the great interpreter of God's counsels of love to sinners, Job xxxiii. 23, " One among a thousand," even " the chief among ten thousand," Cant. v. 10. " One chosen out of the people," Psalm lxxxix. 19. One to whom " the Lord hath given the tongue of the learned —to speak a word in season to him that is weary," Isa. l. 4. It is he that is with him, by his Spirit, now, to " convince him of righteousness," John xvi. 8, as he was with him before, to "convince him of sin and of judgment." His work now is, to shew unto him his uprightness, or his righteousness, that is, the interpreter Christ's righteousness; which is the only righteousness, arising from the paying of a ransom, and upon which a sinner is delivered from going down to the pit, ver. 24. Thus Christ is said to declare God's name, Psalm xxii. 22, and to preach righteousness, Psalm xl. 9. The phrase is remarkable: it is not to shew unto the man, but unto man, his righteousness: which not obscurely intimates, that he is more than a man, who shews or declareth this righteousness. Compare Amos iv. 13, "He that formeth the mountains, and createth the wind, and declareth unto man what is his thought." There seems to be in it a sweet allusion to the first declaration of this righteousness unto man, or, as the word is, unto Adam, after the fall, while he lay under terror from apprehensions of the wrath of God; which declaration was made by the messenger, the interpreter, namely, the eternal *Word*, the Son of God, called, the voice of the Lord God, Gen. iii. 8, and by him appearing, probably, in human shape. Now, while he by his Spirit, is the preacher of righteousness to the man, it is supposed that the man lays hold on the offered righteousness; whereupon the ransom is applied to him, and he is delivered from going down to the pit; for God hath a ransom for him. This is intimated to him by the words, "Deliver him," Job xxxiii. 24. So his conscience being purified by the blood of atonement, is pacified, and sweetly quieted. " He shall pray unto God—and see his face with joy," which before he beheld with horror, ver. 26; that is in New Testament language, " Having an high priest over the house of God," he shall " draw near with a true heart, in full assurance of faith, having his heart sprinkled from an evil conscience," Heb. x. 21, 22. But then, what becomes of the body, the weak and weary flesh? Why, " his flesh shall be fresher than a child's, he shall return to the days of his youth," ver. 25. Yea, " All his bones," which were chastened with strong pain, ver. 19, " shall say, Lord, who is like unto thee?" Psalm xxxv. 10.

A third benefit flowing from union with Christ, is adoption. Believers, being united to Christ, become children of God, and members of the family of heaven. By their union with him, who is the Son of God by nature, they become the sons of God by grace, John i. 12. As when a branch is cut off from one tree, and grafted in the branch of another, the ingrafted branch, by means of its union with the adopting branch, as some not unfitly have called it, is made a branch of the same stock with that into which it is ingrafted: so sinners, being ingrafted into Jesus Christ, whose name is the *Branch*, his Father is their Father, his God their God, John xx. 17. And thus they, who are by nature children of the devil, become the children of God. They have the Spirit of adoption, Rom. viii. 15, namely, the Spirit of his Son, which brings them to God, as children to a Father; to pour out their complaints in his bosom, and to seek necessary supplies, Gal. iv. 6, " Because ye are sons, God has sent forth the Spirit of his Son into your hearts, crying, Abba, Father." Under all their weaknesses, they have fatherly pity and compassion shewn them, Psalm ciii. 13, " Like as a father pitieth his children; so the Lord pitieth them that fear him."—Although they were but foundlings, found in a desert land; yet now " he keeps them as the apple of his eye," Deut. xxxii. 10. Whosoever pursues them, they have a refuge, Prov. xiv. 26, " His children shall have a place of refuge." In a time of common calamity, they have chambers of protection, where they may be hid until the indignation is overpast, Isa. xxvi. 20. And he is not only their refuge for protection, but their portion for provision, in that refuge; Psalm cxlii. 5, " Thou art my refuge, and my portion in the land of the living."—They are provided for, for eternity, Heb. xi. 16, " He hath prepared for them a city." And what he sees they have need of for time, they shall not want, Matt. vi. 31, 32, "Take no thought, saying, What shall we eat? or what shall we drink? or wherewithal shall we be clothed? For your heavenly Father knoweth that ye have need of all these things." Seasonable correction is likewise their privilege as sons: so they are not suffered to pass with their faults, as others who are not children, but servants of the family, who at length will be turned out of doors for their miscarriages, Heb. xii. 7, " If ye endure chastening, God dealeth with you as with sons; for what son is he whom the father chasteneth not? They are heirs of, and shall inherit the promises, Heb. vi. 12. Nay, they are heirs of God, who himself is the portion of their inheritance, Psalm xvi. 5, "and joint-heirs with Christ," Rom. viii. 17. And because they are the children of the great King, and heirs of glory, they have angels for their attendants, who are sent forth to minister for them who shall be heirs of salvation," Heb. i. 14.

A fourth benefit is sanctification, 1 Cor. i. 30, " But of him are ye in Christ Jesus, who of God is made unto us wisdom, and righteousness, and sanctification."—Being united to Christ, they partake of his Spirit, which is the Spirit of holiness. There is a fulness of the Spirit in Christ, and it is not like the fulness of a vessel, which only retains what is poured into it; but it is the fulness of a fountain for diffusion and communication, which is always sending forth its waters, and yet is always full. The Spirit of Christ, that spiritual sap, which is in the stock, and from thence is communicated to the branches, is the Spirit of grace, Zech. xii. 10. And where the Spirit of grace dwells, there will be found a confluence of all graces. Holiness is not one grace only, but all the graces of the Spirit; it is a constellation of graces; it is all the graces in their seed and root. And as the sap conveyed from the stock into the branch goes through it, and through every part of it; so the Spirit of Christ sanctifies the whole man. The poison of sin was diffused through the whole spirit, soul, and body of the man; and sanctifying grace pursues it into every corner, 1 Thess. v. 23. Every part of the man is sanctified, though no part is perfectly so. The truth we are sanctified by is not held in the head, as in a prison; but runs, with its sanctifying influences, through heart and life. There are indeed some graces, in every believer, which appear as top-branches above the rest: as meekness in Moses, patience in Job; but seeing there is in every child of God, a holy principle going along with the holy law, in all the parts thereof, loving and approving of it: as it appears from their universal respect to the commands of God: it is evident that they are endowed with all the graces of the Spirit; because there cannot be less in the effect, than there was in the cause.

Now, this sanctifying Spirit, whereof believers partake, is unto them, 1. A spirit of mortification; " through the Spirit they mortify the deeds of the body," Rom. viii. 13. Sin is crucified in them, Gal. v. 24. They are planted together, namely, with Christ in the likeness of his death, which was a lingering death, Rom. vi. 5. Sin in the saint, though not quite dead, yet is dying. If it were dead, it would be taken down from the cross, and buried out of his sight: but it hangs there as yet, working and struggling under its mortal wounds. As, when a tree has got such a stroke as reaches the heart of it, all the leaves and branches begin to fade and decay: so, where the sanctifying Spirit comes, and breaks the power of sin, there is a gradual ceasing from it, and dying to it, in the whole man; so that he " no longer lives in the flesh to the lusts of men." He does not make sin his trade and business; it is not his great design to seek himself, and to satisfy his corrupt inclinations: but he is seeking for Immanuel's land; and is walking in the highway to it, the way which is called the way of holiness: though the wind from hell, that was on his back before, blows now full in his face, makes his travelling uneasy, and often drives him off the highway. 2. This Spirit is a Spirit of vivification to them; for he is the Spirit of life, and makes them live unto righteousness, Ezek. xxxvi. 27, " And I will put my Spirit within you, and cause you to walk in my statutes." Those who have been "planted together," with Christ, " in the likeness of his death, shall be also in the likeness of his resurrection," Rom. vi. 5. At Christ's resurrection, when his soul was re-united with his body, every member of that blessed body was enabled again to perform the actions of life: so the soul, being influenced by the sanctifying Spirit of Christ, is enabled more and more to perform all the actions of spiritual life. And as the whole of the law, and not some scraps of it only, is written on the holy heart; so believers are enabled to transcribe that law, in their conversation. Although they cannot write one line of it without blots, yet God, for Christ's sake, accepts of the performance, in point of sanctification; they being disciples to his own Son, and led by his own Spirit.

This sanctified Spirit, communicated by the Lord Jesus to his members, is the spiritual nourishment the branches have from the stock into which they are ingrafted; whereby the life of grace, given them in regeneration, is preserved, continued, and actuated. It is the nourishment whereby the new creature lives, and is nourished up towards perfection. Spiritual life needs to be fed, and must have supply of nourishment: and believers derive the same from Christ their head, whom the Father has appointed the head of influence to all his members, Col. ii. 19, "And not holding the head, from which all the body, by joints and bands, having nourishment ministered, or supplied," &c. Now this supply is "the supply of the Spirit of Jesus Christ," Phil. i. 19. The saints feed richly, "eating Christ's flesh, and drinking his blood," for their spiritual nourishment: yet our Lord himself teacheth us, that "it is the Spirit that quickeneth," John vi. 63, even that Spirit who dwells in his blessed body. The human nature is united to the divine nature, in the person of the Son, and so like the bowl in Zachariah's candlestick, chap. iv. lies at the fountain head, as the glorious means of conveyance of influences from the fountain of Deity. He receives not the Spirit by measure, but ever hath a fulness of the Spirit, by reason of that personal union. Hence believers, being united to the man Christ, as the seven lamps to the bowl, by their seven pipes, Zech. iv. 2, his flesh is to them meat indeed, and his blood drink indeed: for, feeding on that blessed body, that is, effectually applying Christ to their souls by faith, they partake more and more of that Spirit, who dwelleth therein, to their spiritual nourishment. The holiness of God can never admit of an immediate union with the sinful creature, nor, consequently, an immediate communion with it: yet the creature could not live the life of grace without communion with the fountain of life. Therefore, that the honour of God's holiness and the salvation of sinners might jointly be provided for, the second person of the glorious trinity took into a personal union with himself a sinless human nature; that so this holy, harmless, and undefiled humanity, might immediately receive a fulness of the Spirit, of which he might communicate to his members, by his divine power and efficacy. Suppose there were a tree, with its root in the earth, and its branches reaching to heaven, the vast distance between the root and the branches, would not interrupt the communication between the root and the top branch: even so, the distance between the man Christ, who is in heaven, and his members, who are on earth, cannot hinder the communication between them. What though the parts of mystical Christ, namely the head and the members, are not contiguous, as joined together in the way of corporal union; the union is not therefore the less real and effectual. Yea, our Lord himself shews us, that though we eat his flesh in a corporeal and carnal manner, yet it would profit nothing, John vi. 63; we should not be one whit the holier thereby. But the members of Christ on earth, are united to their head in heaven, by the invisible bond of the self-same Spirit dwelling in both; in him as the head, and in them as the members. The wheels in Ezekiel's vision were not contiguous to the living creatures, yet were united to them by an invisible bond of one Spirit in both; so that, "when the living creatures went, the wheels went by them, and when the living creatures were lifted up from the earth, the wheels were lifted up," Ezek. i. 19; "For," says the prophet, "the Spirit of the living creature was in the wheels," ver. 20.

Hence we may see the difference between true satisfaction, and that shadow of it, which is to be found among some strict professors of Christianity, who yet are not true Christians, are not regenerated by the Spirit of Christ, and is of the same kind with what has appeared in many sober heathens. True sanctification is the result of the soul's union with the holy Jesus, the first and immediate receptacle of the sanctifying Spirit; out of whose fulness his members do by virtue of their union with him, receive sanctifying influences. The other is the mere product of the man's own spirit, which, whatever it has, or seems to have, of the matter of true holiness, yet does not arise from the supernatural principles, nor to the high aims and ends thereof; for, as it comes from self, so it runs out into the dead sea of self again; and lies as wide of true holiness, as nature doth of grace. They who have this species of holiness, are like common boatmen, who serve themselves with their own oars: whereas the ship bound for Immanuel's land, sails by the blowings of the divine Spirit. How is it possible there should be true satisfaction without Christ? Can there be true sanctification without partaking of the Spirit of holiness? Can we partake of that Spirit, but by Jesus Christ, "the way, the truth, and the life?" The falling dew shall as soon make its way through the flinty rock, as the influences of grace come from God to sinners, any other way than through him whom the Father hath appointed the head of influences, Col. i. 19, "For it pleased the Father, that in him should all fulness dwell:" and chap. ii. 19, "And not holding the head, from which all the body, by joints and bands, having nourishment ministered and knit together, increaseth with the increase of God." Hence see how it comes to pass, that many fall away from their seeming sanctification, and never recover: it is because they are not branches truly knit to the true vine. Meanwhile others, recover from their decays, because of their union with the life-giving stock, by the quickening Spirit, 1 John ii. 19, "They went out from us, but they were not of us; for if they had been of us, they would no doubt have continued with us."

A fifth benefit is growth in grace. "Having nourishment ministered, they increase with the increase of God." Col. ii. 19, "The righteous shall flourish like the palm-tree: he shall grow like a cedar in Lebanon," Psalm xcii. 12. Grace is of a growing nature; in the way to Zion they go from strength to strength. Though the holy man be at first a little child in grace, yet at length he becomes a young man; a father, 1 John ii. 13. Though he does but creep in the way to heaven sometimes, yet afterwards he walks, he runs, he mounts up with wings as eagles, Isa. xl. 31. If a branch grafted into a stock never grows, it is a plain evidence of its not having knit with the stock.

But some perhaps may say, "If all true Christians be growing ones, what shall be said of those who, instead of growing, are going back?" I answer, There is a great difference between the Christians growing simply, and his growing at all times. All true Christians do grow, but I do not say that they grow at all times. A tree, that has life and nourishment, grows to its perfection, yet it is not always growing; it grows not in the winter. Christians also have their winters, wherein the influences of grace, necessary for their growth, cease, Cant. v. 2, "I sleep." It is by faith the believer derives gracious influences from Jesus Christ; as each lamp in the candlestick received oil from the bowel, by the pipe going between them, Zech. iv. 2. Now, if that pipe be stoped, if the saint's faith lie dormant and inactive, then all the rest of the graces will become dim, and seem ready to be extinguished. In consequence whereof, depraved nature will gather strength, and become active. What then will become of the soul? Why, there is still one sure ground of hope. The saint's faith is not as the hypocrite's like a pipe laid short of the fountain, whereby there can be no conveyance: it still remains a bond of union between Christ and the soul; and therefore, because Christ lives, the believer shall live also, John xiv. 19. The Lord Jesus "puts in his hand by the hole of the door," and clears the means of conveyance; and then influences for growth flow, and the believer's graces look fresh and green again, Hos. xiv. 7, "They that dwell under his shadow shall return: they shall revive as the corn, and grow as the vine." In the worst of times, the saints have a principle of growth in them, 1 John iii. 9, "His seed remaineth in him." Therefore, after decays, they revive again: namely, when the winter is over, and the Sun of righteousness returns to them with his warm influences. Mud thrown into a pool may lie there at ease; but if it be cast into a fountain, the spring will at length work it out, and run as clear as formerly. *Secondly,* Christians may mistake their growth, and that two ways. 1. By judging of their case according to their present feeling. They observe themselves, and cannot perceive themselves to be growing; but there is no reason thence to conclude they are not growing, Mark iv. 27, "The seed springs and grows up, he knoweth not how." Were a person to fix his eye ever so stedfastly on a growing tree, he would not see it growing; but if he compare the tree as it now is, with what it was some years ago, he will certainly perceive that it has grown. In like manner may the Christian know whether he be in a growing or declining state, by comparing his present with his former condition. 2. Christians may mistake their case, by measuring their growth by the advances of the top only, not of the root. Though a man be not growing taller, he may be growing stronger. If a tree be uniting with the ground, fixing itself in the earth, and spreading out its roots, it is certainly growing, although it be not higher than formerly. So, although a Christian may want the sweet consolations and flashes of affection which he had; yet, if he be growing in humility, self-denial, and sense of needy dependence on Jesus Christ, he is a growing Christian, Hos. xiv. 5, " I will be as the dew unto Israel, he shall cast forth his roots as Lebanon."

Question. "But do hypocrites grow at all? And if so, how shall we distinguish between their growth, and true Christian growth?" *Answer.* To the first part of the question, hypocrites do grow. The tares have their growth, as well as the wheat: the seed that fell among thorns did spring up, Luke viii. 7. Only it brought no fruit to perfection, ver. 14. Yea, a true Christian may have a false growth. James and John seemed to grow in the grace of holy zeal, when their spirits grew so hot in the cause of Christ, that they would have fired a whole village, for not receiving their Lord and Master, Luke ix. 54, " They said, Lord, wilt thou that we command fire to come down from heaven and consume them, even as Elias did?" But it was indeed no such thing; and therefore he turned and rebuked them, ver. 55, " and said, " Ye know not what manner of spirit ye are of." To the second part of the question it is answered, that there is a peculiar beauty in the true Christian growth, distinguishing it from all false growth: it is universal, regular, proportionable. It is a "growing up into Him in all things, which is the head," Eph. iv. 15. The growing Christian grows proportionably, in all the parts of the new man. Under the kindly influences of the Sun of righteousness, believers "grow up as calves of the stall," Mal. iv. 2. You would think it a monstrous growth, in these creatures, if you saw their heads grow, and not their bodies; or if you saw one leg grow, and another not; if all the parts do not grow proportionably. Ay, but such is the growth of many in religion. They grow like rickety children, who have a big head, but a slender body; they get more knowledge into their heads, but no more holiness into their hearts and lives. They grow very hot outwardly, but very cold inwardly; like men in a fit of the ague. They are more taken up about the externals of religion than formerly; yet as great strangers to the power of godliness as ever. If a garden is watered with the hand, some of the plants will readily get much, some little, and some no water at all; and therefore some wither, while others are coming forward; but after a shower from the clouds, all come forward together. In like manner, all the graces of the Spirit grow proportionably, by the special influences of divine grace. The branches ingrafted in Christ, growing aright, do grow in all the several ways of growth at once. They grow inward, growing into Christ, Eph. iv. 15, uniting more closely with him; and cleaving more firmly to him, as the head of influences, which is the spring of all other true Christian growth. They grow outward in good works, in their life and conversation. They not only, with Naphtali, give goodly words; but, like Joseph, they are fruitful boughs. They grow upward in heavenly-mindedness, and contempt of the world; for their conversation is in heaven, Phil. iii. 20. And finally, they grow downward in humility and self-loathing. The branches of the largest growth in Christ, are, in their own eyes, "less than the least of all saints," Eph. iii. 8; "the chief of sinners," 1 Tim. i. 15; "more brutish than any man," Prov. xxx. 2. They see that they can do nothing, no, not so much as "think any thing, as of themselves," 2 Cor. iii. 5 : that they deserve nothing, being "not worthy of the least of all the mercies showed unto them," Gen. xxxii. 10; and that they are nothing, 2 Cor. xii. 11.

A sixth benefit is fruitfulness. The branch ingrafted into Christ is not barren, but brings forth fruit, John xv. 5, "He that abideth in me, and I in him, the same bringeth forth much fruit." For that very end are souls united to Christ, that they may bring forth fruit unto God, Rom. vii. 4. They that are barren may be branches in Christ by profession, but not by real implantation. Whoever are united to Christ, bring forth the fruit of gospel-obedience and true holiness. Faith is always followed with good works. The believer is not only come out of the grave of his natural state; but he has put off his grave-clothes, namely, reigning lusts, in which he walked, like a ghost; being dead while he lived in them, Col. iii. 7, 8. For Christ has said of him, as of Lazarus, " Loose him, and let him go." Now that he has put on Christ, he personates him, so to speak, as a beggar in borrowed robes represents a king on the stage, walking as he also walked. Now the fruit of the Spirit in him, is in all goodness, Eph. v. 9. The fruits of holiness will be found in the hearts, lips, and lives of those who are united to Christ. The hidden man of the heart is not only a temple built for God, and consecrated to him; but used and employed for him, where love, fear, trust, and all the other parts of unseen religion, are exercised, Phil. iii. 3, " For we are the circumcision which worship God in the Spirit." The heart is no more the devil's common, where thoughts go free; for there even vain thoughts are hated, Psalm cxix. 113. But it is God's enclosure, hedged about as a garden for him, Cant. iv. 16. It is true, there are weeds of corruption there, because the ground is not yet perfectly cleared: but the man, in the day of his new creation, is set to dress it, and keep it. A live coal from the altar has touched his lips, and they are purified. Psalm xv. 1—3, " Lord, who shall abide in thy tabernacle? who shall dwell in thy holy hill? He that speaketh the truth in his heart; he that backbiteth not with his tongue, nor taketh up a reproach against his neighbour." There may be, indeed, a smooth tongue, where there is a false heart. The voice may be Jacob's, while the hand's are Esau's. But, " if any man among you seem to be religious, and bridleth not his tongue, but deceiveth his own heart, this man's religion is vain," James i. 26. The power of godliness will rule over the tongue, though a world of iniquity. If one be a Galilean, his speech will bewray him; he will speak, not the language of Ashdod, but the language of Canaan. He will neither be dumb in religion, nor will his tongue walk at random, seeing, to the double guard which nature hath given the tongue, grace hath added a third. The fruits of holiness will be found in his outward conversation; for he hath clean hands, as well as a pure heart, Psalm xxiv. 4. He is a godly man, and religiously discharges the duties of the first table of the law; he is a righteous man, and honestly performs the duties of the second table. In his conversation he is a good Christian, and a good neighbour too. He carries it towards God, as if men's eyes were upon him; and towards men, as believing God's eyes to be upon him. Those things which God hath joined in his law, he dares not put asunder in his practice.

Thus the branches in Christ are full of good fruits. And those fruits are a cluster of vital actions, whereof Jesus Christ is the principle and end. The principle; for he lives in them, and " the life they live is by faith in the Son of God," Gal. ii. 20. The end; for they live to him, and "to them to live is Christ," Phil. i. 21. The duties of religion are in the world, like fatherless children, in rags; some will not take them in, because they never loved them nor their Father; some take them in, because they may be serviceable to them: but the saints take them in for their Father's sake, that is for Christ's sake: and they are lovely in their eyes, because they are like him. O! whence is this new life of the saints? Surely it could never have been hammered out of the natural powers of their souls, by the united force of all created power. In eternal barrenness would they have continued; but that being "married to Christ, they bring forth fruit unto God," Rom. vii. 4.

If you ask me, "How can your nourishment, growth, and fruitfulness be forwarded?" I offer these few advices: 1. Make sure work, as to your knitting with the stock by faith unfeigned; and beware of hypocrisy: a branch that is not sound at the heart will certainly wither. The trees of the Lord's planting are trees of righteousness, Isa. lxi. 3. So, when others fade, they bring forth fruit. Hypocrisy is a disease in the vitals of religion, which will consume all at length. It is a leak in the ship, that will certainly sink it. Sincerity of grace will make it lasting, be it ever so weak; as the smallest twig, that is sound at the heart, will draw nourishment from the stock and grow; while the greatest bough that is rotten can never recover, because it receives no nourishment. 2. Labour to be stedfast in the truths and way of God. An unsettled and wavering judgment is a great enemy to Christian growth and fruitfulness, as the apostle teaches, Eph. iv. 14, 15, "That we henceforth be no more children, tossed to and fro, and carried about with every wind of doctrine. But speaking the truth in love, may grow up into him in all things, which is the head, even Christ." A rolling stone gathers no moss, and a wavering judgment makes a fruitless life. Though a tree be never so sound, yet how can it grow, or be fruitful, if you be still removing it out of one soil into another? 3. Endeavour to cut off the suckers, as gardeners do, that their trees may thrive. These are unmortified lusts; therefore "mortify your members that are upon the earth," Col. iii. 5. When the Israelites got meat to their lusts, they got leanness to their souls. She that has many hungry children about her hand, and must be still putting into their mouths, will have much ado to get a bit put into her own. They must refuse the cravings of inordinate affections, who would have their souls to prosper. 4. Improve, for these ends, the ordinances of God. It is in the courts of our God where the trees of righteousness flourish, Psalm xcii. 13. The waters of the sanctuary are the means appointed of God, to cause his people to grow as willows by the water courses. Therefore drink in with "desire, the sincere milk of the word, that ye may grow thereby," 1 Pet. ii. 2. Come to these wells of salvation: not to look at them only, but to draw water out of them. The sacrament of the Lord's supper is in a special manner appointed for these ends. It is not only a solemn public profession, and a seal of our union and communion with Christ; but it is a means of most intimate communion with him; and strengthens our union with him, our faith, love, repentance, and other graces, 1 Cor. x. 16, "The cup of blessing, which we bless, is it not the communion of the blood of Christ? The bread which we break, it is not the communion of the body of Christ?" And chap. xii. 13, "We have been all made to drink into one Spirit." Give yourselves unto prayer; open your mouths wide, and he will fill them.—By these means the branches in Christ may be farther nourished, grow up, and bring forth much fruit.

A seventh benefit is, The acceptance of their fruits of holiness before the Lord. Though they may be very imperfect, they are accepted, because they savour of Christ the blessed stock, which the branches grow upon; while the fruits of others are rejected of God, Gen. iv. 4, 5, "And the Lord had respect unto Abel, and his offering; but unto Cain and his offering he had no respect." Compare Heb. xi. 3, "By faith, Abel offered unto God a more excellent sacrifice than Cain." O how defective are the saints' duties in the eye of the law! The believer himself sees many faults in his best performances; yet the Lord graciously receives them.—There is no grace planted in the heart, but there is a weed of corruption hard by its side, while the saints are in the lower world. Their very sincerity is not without a mixture of dissimulation or hypocrisy, Gal. ii. 13. Hence there are defects in the exercise of every grace; in the performance of every duty; depraved nature always drops something to stain their best works. There is still a mixture of darkness with their clearest light. Yet this does not mar their acceptance, Cant. vi. 10, "Who is she that looketh forth as the morning?" or, as the dawning? Behold how Christ's spouse is esteemed and accepted of her Lord, even when she looks forth as the morning, whose beauty is mixed with the blackness of the night! "When the morning was looking out," as the word is Jud. xix. 26, that is, "In the dawning of the day," as we read it. So the very dawning of grace, and good will to Christ, grace peeping out from under a mass of darkness in believers, is pleasant and acceptable to him, as the break of day is to the weary traveller.—Though the remains of unbelief make the hand of faith to shake and tremble; yet the

Lord is so well pleased with it, that he employs it to carry away pardons and supplies of grace, from the throne of grace, and the fountain of grace. His faith was effectual, "who " cried out and said with tears, Lord, I believe, help thou mine unbelief!" Mark ix. 24. Though the remains of sensual affections make the flame of their love weak and smoky; he turns his eyes from the smoke, and beholds the flame, how fair it is, Cant. iv. 10, "How fair is thy love, my sister, my spouse!"—"The smell of their" under "garment" of inherent holiness, as imperfect as it is, "is like the smell of Lebanon," ver. 11; and that because they are covered with their elder brother's clothes, which makes the sons of God to "smell as a field which the Lord hath blessed." Their good works are accepted: their cups of cold water given to a disciple, in the name of a disciple, shall not want a reward. Though they cannot offer for the tabernacle, gold, silver, and brass, and onyx stones, let them come forward with what they have; if it were but goats' hair, it shall not be rejected; if it were but ram's skins, they shall be kindly accepted; for they are dyed red, dipt by faith in the Mediator's blood, and so presented unto God. A very ordinary work done in faith, and from faith, if it were but the building of a wall about the holy city, is a great work, Neh. vi. 3. If it were but the bestowing of a box of ointment on Christ, it shall never be forgotten, Matt. xxvi. 13. Even "a cup of cold water only given to one of Christ's little ones, in the name of a disciple, shall be rewarded," Matt. x. 42. Nay, not a good word for Christ shall drop from their mouths, but it shall be registered in God's "book of remembrance," Mal. iii. 16. Nor shall a tear drop from their eyes for him, but he will "put it in his bottle," Psalm lvi. 8. Their will is accepted for the deed; their sorrow for the want of will, for the will itself, 2 Cor. viii. 12, "For if there be first a willing mind, it is accepted according to that a man hath, and not according to that he hath not." Their groanings, when they cannot well express their desires, are heard in heaven; the meaning of those groans is well known there, and they will be returned like the dove with an olive branch of peace in her mouth. See Rom. viii. 26, 27. Their mites are better than other men's talents. Their lisping and broken sentences are more pleasant to their Father in heaven, than the most fluent or flourishing speeches of those who are not in Christ. Their voice is sweet, even when they are ashamed it should be heard; their countenance is comely, even when they blush, and draw a veil over it, Cant. ii. 14. The Mediator takes their petitions, blots out some parts, rectifies others, and then presents them to the Father, in consequence whereof they pass in the court of heaven.

Every true Christian is a temple to God. If you look for sacrifices, they are not wanting there; they offer the sacrifice of praise, and do good: with such sacrifices God is well pleased, Heb. xiii. 15, 16. Christ himself is the altar that sanctifies the gift, ver. 10. If we look for incense, it is there too. The graces of the Spirit are found in their hearts: and the Spirit of the crucified Christ fires them, and puts them in exercise; as the fire was brought from the altar of burnt-offering, to set the incense in flame: then they mount heavenward, like pillars of smoke, Cant. iii. 6. But the best of incense will leave ashes behind it: yes, indeed; but as the priest took away the ashes of the incense in a golden dish, and threw them out; so our great High Priest takes away the ashes and refuse of all the saint's services, by his mediation in their behalf.

An eighth benefit flowing from union with Christ, is establishment. The Christian cannot fall away, but must persevere unto the end, John x. 28, "they shall never perish, neither shall any man pluck them out of my hand." Indeed, if a branch do not knit with the stock, it will fall away when shaking winds arise: but the branch knit to the stock stands fast whatever wind blows. Sometimes a stormy wind of temptation blows from hell, and shakes the branches in Christ the true vine: but their union with him is their security; moved they may be, but removed they never can be.— The Lord "will with the temptation also make a way of escape," 1 Cor. x. 13. Calms are never of any continuance; there is almost always some wind blowing; and therefore branches are rarely altogether at rest. But sometimes violent winds arise, which threaten to rend them from off their stock. Even so it is with saints; they are daily put to it to keep their ground against temptation: sometimes the wind from hell rises so high, and blows so furiously, that it makes even top branches to sweep the ground; yet being knit to Christ their stock, they get up again, in spite of the most violent efforts of the prince of the power of the air, Psalm xciv. 18, "When I said, my foot slippeth, thy mercy, O Lord, held me up." But the Christian improves by his trial; and is so far from being damaged, that he is benefited by it, as it discovers what hold the soul has of Christ, and what hold Christ has of the soul. And look, as the wind in the bellows, which would blow out the candle, blows up the fire; even so it often comes to pass, that such temptations enliven the true Christian, awakening the graces of the Spirit in him; and by that means, discover both the reality and the strength of grace in him. And hence, as Luther, that great man of God, saith, "One Christian, who hath had experience of temptation, is worth a thousand others."

Sometimes a stormy wind of trouble and persecution from the men of the world, blows upon the vine, that is, mystical Christ; but union with the stock is a sufficient security to the branches. In a time of the church's peace and outward prosperity, while the angels hold the winds that they blow not, there are a great many branches taken up and put into the stock, which never knit with it, nor live by it, though they be bound up with it by the bonds of external ordinances. Now, these may stand a while on the stock, and stand with great ease while the calm lasts; but when once the storms arise, and the winds blow, they will begin to fall off one after another; and the higher the wind rises, the greater will the number be that falls. Yea, some strong boughs of that sort, when they fall, will, by their weight, carry others of their own kind, quite down to the earth with them; and will bruise and press down some true branches in such a manner, that they would also fall off, were it not for that fast hold which the stock has of them. Then it is that many branches which before were high and eminent, are found lying on the earth withered, and fit to be gathered up and cast into the fire, Matt. xiii. 6, "When the sun was up, they were scorched: and because they had no root, they withered away." John xv. 6, "If a man abide not in me, he is cast forth as a branch, and is withered and men gather them, and cast them into the fire, and they are burned." But however violently the winds blow, none of the truly ingrafted branches that are knit with the stock are found missing, when the storm is changed into a calm, John xvii. 12, "Those that thou gavest me, I have kept, and none of them is lost." The least twig growing in Christ shall stand it out, and subsist; when the tallest cedars growing on their own root, shall be laid flat on the ground, Rom. viii. 35, "Who shall separate us from the love of Christ? Shall tribulation, or distress, or persecution, or famine, or nakedness, or peril, or sword?" See ver. 36—39. However severely Israel be "sifted, yet shall not the least grain," or, as it is in the original language, a little stone, "fall upon the earth," Amos ix. 9. It is an allusion to the sifting of fine pebble stones from among heaps of dust and sand: though the sand and dust fall to the ground be blown away with the wind, and trampled under foot; yet there shall not fall on the earth so much as a little stone, such is the exactness of the seive, and the care of the sifter.—There is nothing more ready to fall on the earth than a stone: yet, if professors of religion be lively stones, built on Christ the chief corner-stone, although they be little stones, they shall not fall to the earth, whatever storm beats upon them. See 1 Pet. ii. 4—6. All the good grain in the church of Christ is of this kind: they are stones, in respect of solidity;

and lively stones in respect of activity. If men be solid substantial Christians, they will not be like chaff tossed to and fro with every wind; having so much of the liveliness, that they have nothing of the stone: and if they be lively Christians, whose spirits will stir in them, as Paul's did, when he saw the city wholly given to idolatry, Acts xvii. 16, they will not lie like stones, to be turned over, hither and thither, cut and carved, according to the lusts of men; having so much of the stone, as leaves nothing of liveliness in them.

Our God's house is a great house, wherein are not only vessels of gold, but also of earth, 2 Tim. ii. 20.—Both these are apt to contract filthiness; and therefore when God brings trouble upon the church, he hath an eye to both. As for the vessels of gold, they are not destroyed; but purified by a fiery trial in the furnace of affliction, as goldsmiths refine their gold, Isa. i. 25, "And I will turn my hand upon thee, and purely purge away thy dross." But destruction is to the vessels of earth; they shall be broken in shivers, as a potter's vessel, ver. 28, " And the destruction," or breaking " of the transgressors, and of the sinners, shall be together." It seems to be an allusion to that law, for breaking the vessels of earth, when unclean; while vessels of wood, and consequently vessels of gold, were only to be rinsed, Lev. xv. 12.

A ninth benefit is support. If thou be a branch ingrafted in Christ, the root beareth thee. The believer leans on Christ, as a weak woman in a journey leaning upon her beloved husband, Cant. viii. 5. He stays himself upon him, as a feeble old man stays himself on his staff, Isa. l. 10. He rolls himself on him, as one rolls a burden he is not able to walk under, off his own back, upon another who is able to bear it, Psal. xxii. 8, marg. There are many weights to hang upon and press down the branches in Christ the true vine. But you know, whatever weights hang on the branches, the stock bears all; it bears the branch, and the weight that is upon it too.

1. Christ supports believers in him, under a weight of outward troubles. That is a large promise, Isa. xliii. 2, " When thou passest through the waters, I will be with thee: and through the rivers they shall not overflow thee." See how David was supported under a heavy load, 1 Sam. xxx. 6. His city Ziglag was burnt, his wives were taken captives, his men spoke of stoning him: nothing was left him but his God and his faith; but by his faith, he encouraged himself in his God. The Lord comes, and lays his cross on his people's shoulders; it presses them down, and they are likely to sink under it, and therefore cry, " Master, save us, we perish;" but he supports them under their burden; he bears them up, and they bear their cross. Thus the Christian, with a weight of outward

troubles upon him, goes lightly under his burden, having the everlasting arms underneath him. The Christian has a spring of comfort, which he cannot lose; and therefore never wants something to support him. If a man have all his riches in money, robbers may take these away; and then what has he more? But though the landed proprietor may be robbed of his money, yet his lands remain for his support. Those who build their comfort on worldly goods, may quickly be comfortless; but those who are united to Christ shall find comfort, when all the streams of worldly enjoyments are dried up, Job vi. 13, "Is not my help in me? and is wisdom driven quite from me?" that is, Though my substance is gone; though my servants, my children, my health, and soundness of body, are all gone; yet my grace is not gone too. Though the Sabeans have driven away my oxen and asses, and the Chaldeans have driven away my camels; they have not driven away my faith, and my hope too: these are yet in me; they are not driven from me; so that by them I can fetch comfort from heaven, when I can have none from earth.

2. Christ supports his people under a weight of inward troubles and discouragements. Many times "heart and flesh fail them;" but then "God is the strength of their heart," Psalm lxxxiii. 26. They may have a weight of guilt pressing them. This is a load that will make their backs bend, and their spirits sink: but he takes it off, and puts a pardon into their hand, while they cast their burden upon him. Christ takes the soul, as one marries a widow under a burden of debt: and so when the creditors come to Christ's spouse, she carries them to her husband, confesses the debt, declares she is not able to pay, and lays all upon him. The Christian sometimes, through carelessness, losses his discharge; he cannot find it, however he search for it. The law takes that opportunity, and proceeds against him for a debt paid already. God hides his face, and the soul is distressed. Many arrows go through the heart now; many long accounts are laid before the man, which he reads and acknowledges. Often does he see the officers coming to apprehend him, and the prison door open to receive him. What else keeps him from sinking utterly under discouragements in this case, but the everlasting arms of a Mediator underneath him, and that he relies upon the great Surety. Farther, they may have a weight of strong lusts pressing them. They have a body of death upon them. Death is a weight that presses the soul out of the body. A leg or an arm of death, if I may so speak, would be a terrible load. One lively lust will sometimes lie so heavy on a child of God, that he can no more remove it than a child could throw a giant from

off him. How then are they supported under a whole body of death? Their support is from that root which bears them, from the everlasting arm that is underneath them. "His grace is sufficient for them," 2 Cor. xii. 9. The great stay of the believer is not the grace of God within him; that is a well whose streams sometimes run dry: but it is the grace of God without him, the grace that is in Jesus Christ; which is an ever-flowing fountain, to which the believer can never come amiss. For the apostle tells us in the same verse, it is "the power of Christ." "Most gladly therefore," saith he, "will I rather glory in my infirmities, that the power of Christ may rest upon me," or "tabernacle above me," as the cloud of glory did on the Israelites, which God spread for a covering, or shelter, to them in the wilderness, Psalm xv. 39; compare Isa. iv. 5, 6. So that the believer in this combat, like the eagle, first flies aloft by faith, and then comes down on the prey, Psalm xxxiv. 5, "They looked to him, and were lightened." Finally, they have a weight of weakness and wants upon them, but they "cast over that burden on the Lord," their strength, "and he sustains them," Psalm lv. 22. With all their wants and weakness they are cast upon him; as the poor, weak, and naked babe coming out of the womb, is cast into the lap of one appointed to take care of it, Psalm xxii. 10. Though they be destitute, as a shrub in the wilderness, which the foot of every beast may tread down, the Lord will regard them, Psalm cii. 17. It is not surprising that the weakest plant should be safe in a garden: but our Lord Jesus Christ is a hedge for protection to his weak and destitute ones, even in a wilderness.

Objection. "But if the saints be so supported, how is it that they fall so often under temptation and discouragements? *Answer.* 1. How low soever they fall at any time they never fall off; and that is a great matter. They "are kept by the power of God through faith unto salvation," 1 Pet. i. 5. Hypocrites may fall, so as to fall off, and fall into the pit, as a bucket falls into a well when the chain breaks. But, though the child of God may fall, and that so low that the waters go over his head, yet there is still a bond of union between Christ and him; the chain is not broken; he will not go to the ground; he will be drawn up again, Luke xxii. 31, 32, "And the Lord said, Simon, Simon, Satan hath desired to have you, that he may sift you as wheat: but I have prayed for thee, that thy faith fail not." 2. The falls of the saints flow from their not improving their union with Christ, their not making use of him by faith, for staying or bearing them up, Psalm xxvii. 13, "I had fainted, unless I had believed." While the nurse holds the child in her arms, it cannot fall to the ground; yet if the unwary child hold not by her, it may fall backwards in her arms, to its great hurt. Thus David's fall broke his bones, Psalm ii. 8; but it did not break the bond of union between Christ and him; the Holy Spirit, the bond of that union, was not taken from him, ver. 11.

The last benefit I shall name, is, the special care of the Husbandman, John xvi. 1, 2, "I am the true vine, and my Father is the husbandman. Every branch that beareth fruit, he purgeth it, that it may bring forth more fruit." Believers, by virtue of their union with Christ, are the objects of God's special care and providence. Mystical Christ is God's vine; other societies in the world are but wild olive trees. The men of the world are but God's out-field; the saints are his vineyard, which he has a special propriety in, and a special concern for, Cant. viii. 12, "My vineyard, which is mine, is before me." He that slumbers not nor sleeps, is the keeper of it; he does keep it; lest any hurt it, he will keep it night and day; he, in whose hand is the dew of heaven, will water it every moment, Isa. xxvii. 3. He dresses and weeds it, in order to further its fruitfulness, John xv. 2. He cuts off the luxuriant twigs, that mar the fruitfulness of the branch. This is done, especially by the word, and by cross or afflictions; the saints need the ministry of the word, as much as the vineyard needeth one to dress and prune the vines, 1 Cor. iii. 9, "We are labourers together with God; ye are God's husbandry, ye are God's building." And they need the cross too, 1 Pet. i. 6.

Therefore, if we were to reckon the cross amongst the benefits flowing to believers from their union with Christ, I judge that we should not reckon amiss. Sure I am, in their sufferings, they "suffer with him," Rom. viii. 17. The assurances which they have of the cross, have rather the nature of a promise, than of a threatening, Psalm lxxxix. 30—33, "If his children forsake my law— then will I visit their transgression with the rod, and their iniquity with stripes Nevertheless, my loving-kindness will I not utterly take from him, nor suffer my faithfulness to fail." This looks like a tutor's engaging to a dying father, to take care of the children left with him; and to give them both nurture and admonition for their good. The covenant of grace truly beats the spears of affliction into pruning-hooks, to them that are in Christ, Isa. xxviii. 9, "By this therefore shall the iniquity of Jacob be purged, and this is all the fruit to take away his sin." Why then should we be angry with our cross? why should we be frightened at it? The believer must take up his cross, and follow his leader, the Lord Jesus Christ. He must take up his every-day's cross, Luke ix. 23, "If any man will come after me, let him deny himself, and take up his cross daily:" Yea, he must take up holy day's cross too, Lam. ii. 22, "Thou hast called, as in a solemn day, my terrors round about." The church of the Jews had of a long time many a pleasant meeting at the temple, on solemn days, for the worship of God; but they got a solemnity of another nature, when God called together, about the temple and city, the Chaldean army, that burnt the temple, and laid Jerusalem on heaps. And as the church of God is yet militant in this lower region, how can it be but the clouds will return after the rain? But the cross of Christ, by which appellation the saint's troubles are named, is a kindly name to the believer. —It is a cross indeed; not to the believer's graces, but to his corruptions. The hypocrite's seeming grace may indeed breathe out their last on a cross, as those of the stony-ground hearers did, Matt. xiii. 6, "When the sun" of persecution, ver. 21, "was up, they were scorched; and because they had not root, they withered away;" but never did one of the real graces in a believer die upon the cross yet. Nay, as the candle shines brightest in the night, and the fire burns fiercest in intense frost; so the believers graces are commonly most vigorous in a time of trouble.

There is a certain pleasure and sweetness in the cross, to those who have their senses exercised to discern, and to find it out. There is a certain sweetness in a man's seeing himself upon his trial for heaven, and standing candidate for glory. There is a pleasure in travelling over those mountains, where the Christian can see the prints of Christ's own feet, and the footsteps of the flock, who have been there before him. How pleasant is it to a saint, in the exercise of grace, to see how a good God crosses his corrupt inclinations, and prevents his folly! How sweet is it to behold these thieves upon the cross! How refined a pleasure is there in observing how God draws away provision from unruly lusts, and so pinches them, that the Christian may get them governed! Of a truth, there is a paradise within this thorn-hedge. Many a time the people of God are in bonds; which are never loosed, till they are bound with cords of affliction. God takes them, and throws them into a fiery furnace, that burns off their bonds; and then, like the three children, Dan. iii. 25, they are "loose, walking in the midst of the fire." God gives his children a potion, with one bitter ingredient: if they will not work upon them, he will put in a second, a third, and so on, as there is need, that they may work together for their good, Rom. viii. 28. With cross winds he hastens them to their labour. They are often found in such ways, as that the cross is the happiest thing that they can meet with: and well may they salute it as David did Abigail, saying, "Blessed be the Lord God of Israel, which sent thee this day to meet me," 1 Sam. xxv. 32. Worldly things are often such a load to the Christian, that he moves but very slowly heavenward. God sends a wind of trouble, that blows the burden off the man's back; he then walks more speedily on his way; after God has drawn some gilded earth from him, that was drawing his heart away from God, Zeph. iii. 12, "I will also leave in the midst of thee an afflicted and poor people, and they shall trust in the name of the Lord." It was an observation of a heathen moralist, that "no history makes mention of any man, who hath been made better by riches." I doubt whether our modern histories can supply the defect of ancient histories in this point. But sure I am, many have been the worse for riches: thousands have been hugged to death in the embraces of a smiling world; and many good men have got wounds from outward prosperity, that must be cured by the cross. I remember to have read of one, who having an imposthume in his breast, had in vain used the help of physicians: but being wounded with a sword, the imposthume broke; and his life was saved by that accident, which threatened immediate death. Often hath spiritual imposthumes gathered in the breasts of God's people, in time of outward prosperity, and been thus broken and dispersed by the cross. It is kindly for believers to be healed by stripes; although they are usually so weak as to cry out for fear, at the sight of the pruning-hook, as if it were the destroying axe; and to think that the Lord is coming to kill them, when he is indeed coming to cure them.

I shall now conclude, addressing myself in a few words, first, to saints, and next to sinners.

To you that are saints, I say,

First, strive to obtain and keep up actual communion and fellowship with Jesus Christ; that is, to be still deriving fresh supplies of grace, from the fountain thereof in him, by faith: and making suitable returns of them, in the exercise of grace and holy obedience. Beware of estrangement between Christ and your souls. If it has got in already, which seems to be the case of many this day, endeavour to get it removed. There are multitudes in the world who slight Christ, though you should not slight him: many that looked fair for heaven, have turned their backs upon him. The warm sun of outward peace and prosperity, has caused some to cast their cloak of religion from them, who held it fast when the wind of trouble was blowing upon them: and "Will you also go away?" John vi. 67. The basest ingratitude is stamped on your slighting communion with Christ, Jer. ii. 31, "Have I been a wilderness unto Israel, a land of darkness? Wherefore say my people, We are lords, we will come no more unto thee?"—Oh! beloved, "Is this your kindness to your friend?" It is unbecoming any wife to slight converse with her husband, but her especially who was taken from a prison or a dunghill, as you were, by your Lord. It is not a time for you to be out of your chambers, Isa. xxvi. 20. They that now are walking most closely with God, may have enough to do to stand when the trial comes: how hard will it be for others then, who are like to be surprised with troubles, when guilt is lying on their consciences unremoved! To be awakened out of a sound sleep, and cast into a raging sea, as Jonah was, will be a fearful trial. To feel trouble before we see it coming, to be past hope before we have any fear, is a very sad case. Wherefore break down your idols of jealousy, mortify those lusts, those irregular appetites and desires, that have stolen away your hearts, and left you like Samson without his hair, and say, "I will go and return to my first husband; for then was it better with me than now," Hos. ii. 7.

Secondly, Walk as becomes those that are united to Christ. Prove your union with him by "walking as he also walked," 1 John ii. 6. If you are brought from under the power of darkness, let your light shine before men. "Shine as lights in the world, holding forth the word of life;" as the lantern holds the candle, which being in it, shines through it, Phil. ii. 15, 16. Now that you profess Christ to be in you, let his image shine forth in your conversation, and remember that the business of your lives is to prove, by practical arguments, what you profess.

1. You know the character of a wife: "She that is married, careth how she may please her husband."—Go you, and do likewise; "walk worthy of the Lord unto all pleasing," Col. i. 10. This is the great business of life; you must please him, though it should displease all the world. What he hates must be hateful to you, because he hates it. Whatever lusts come to gain your hearts, deny them, seeing the grace of God has appeared, teaching us so to do, and you are joined to the Lord.—Let him be a covering to your eyes; for you have not your choice to make, it is made already; and you must not dishonour your head. A man takes care of his feet, because, if he catch cold there, it flies up to his head.—"Shall I then take the members of Christ, and make them the members of a harlot? God forbid," says the apostle, 1 Cor. vi. 14. Wilt thou take that heart of thine, which is Christ's dwelling-place, and lodge his enemies there? Wilt thou take that body, which is his temple and defile it, by using the members thereof as instruments of sin?

2. Be careful to bring forth fruit, and much fruit. The branch well laden with fruit, is the glory of the vine, and of the husbandman

too, John xv. 8, " Herein is my Father glorified, that ye bear much fruit ; so shall ye be my disciples." A barren tree stands safer in a wood, than in an orchard ; and branches in Christ, that bring not forth fruit will be taken away, and cast into the fire.

3. Be heavenly-minded, and maintain a holy contempt of the world. You are united to Christ; he is your head and husband, and is in heaven ; wherefore your hearts should be there also. Col. iii. 1, " If ye then be risen with Christ, seek those things which are above, where Christ sitteth on the right hand of God." Let the serpent's seed go on their belly, and eat the dust of this earth : but let the members of Christ be ashamed to bow down, and feed with them.

4. Live and act dependently, depending by faith on Jesus Christ. That which grows on its own root, is a tree, not a branch. It is of the nature of a branch, to depend on the stock for all, and to derive all its sap from thence. Depend on him for life, light, strength, and all spiritual benefits, Gal. ii. 20, " I live, yet not I, but Christ liveth in me ; and the life which I live now in the flesh, I live by the faith of the Son of God." For this cause, in the mystical union, strength is united to weakness, that death and earth may mount up on borrowed wings. Depend on him for temporal benefits also; Matt. vi. 11, " Give us this day our daily bread." If we have trusted him with our eternal concerns, let us be ashamed to distrust him in the matter of our provision in the world.

5. Be of a meek disposition, and a uniting temper with the fellow members of Christ's body, as being united to the meek Jesus, the blessed centre of union.—There is a prophecy to this purpose concerning the kingdom of Christ, Isa. xi. 6, " The wolf shall dwell with the lamb ; and the leopard shall lie down with the kid." It is an allusion to the beast's in Noah's ark. The beasts of prey that were wont to kill and devour others, when once they came into the ark, lay down in peace with them : the lamb was in no hazard from the wolf there, nor the kid from the leopard. There was a beautiful accomplishment of it in the primitive church, Acts iv. 32, " And the multitude of them that believed, were of one heart and of one soul." And this prevails in all the members of Christ, according to the measure of the grace of God in them. Man is born naked : he comes naked into this world, as if God designed him for the picture of peace ; and surely, when he is born again, he comes not into the new world of grace with claws to tear, a sword to wound, and a fire in his hand to burn up his fellow-members in Christ, because they cannot see with his light. Oh ! it is sad to see Christ's lilies as thorns in one another's sides, Christ's lambs devouring one another

like lions, and God's diamonds cutting one another: yet it must be
remembered, that sin is no proper cement for the members of Christ,
though Herod and Pontius Pilate may be made friends that way.
The apostle's rule is plain, Heb. xii. 14, "Follow peace with all
men, and holiness." To follow peace no farther than our humour,
credit, and such like things will allow us, is too short: to pursue it
farther than holiness allows us, that is, conformity to the Divine
will, is too far. Peace is precious, yet it may be bought too dearly:
wherefore we must rather want it, than purchase it at any expense
of truth or holiness. But otherwise it cannot be bought too dearly;
and it will always be precious in the eyes of the sons of peace.

And now, sinners, what shall I say to you? I have given you
some view of the privileges of those in the state of grace. You have
seen them afar off; but alas! they are not yours, because you are
not Christ's. The sinfulness of an unregenerate state is yours; and
the misery of it is yours also: you have neither part nor lot in this
matter. The guilt of all your sins lies upon you; you have no part
in the righteousness of Christ. There is no peace to you, no peace
with God, no true peace of conscience; for you have no saving interest in the great peace-maker. You are none of God's family;
the adoption we spoke of, belongs not to you. You have no part in
the Spirit of sanctification; and, in one word, you have no inheritance among them that are sanctified. All I can say to you in this
matter, is, that the case is not desperate, they may yet be yours,
Rev. iii. 20, "Behold, I stand at the door and knock; if any man
hear my voice, and open the door, I will come into him, and will
sup with him, and he with me." Heaven is proposing a union with
earth still; the potter is making suit to his own clay; and the gates
of the city of refuge are not yet closed. O that we could compel
you to come in! Thus far of the state of grace.

www.ingramcontent.com/pod-product-compliance
Lightning Source LLC
Chambersburg PA
CBHW031412040426
42444CB00005B/527